Making Money from Home

Making Money from Home

How to Run a Successful Home-Based Business

donna partow

Tyndale House Publishers, Inc.
CAROL STREAM, ILLINOIS

A Focus on the Family book published by
Tyndale House Publishers, Inc., Carol Stream, Illinois 60188

Focus on the Family and the accompanying logo and design are federally registered trademarks of
Focus on the Family, Colorado Springs, CO 80995.

TYNDALE and Tyndale's quill logo are registered trademarks of Tyndale House Publishers, Inc.

Editor: Marianne Hering
Cover design by Ron Kaufmann
Cover photograph by Kala Ketchum, copyright © 2009 by Focus on the Family. All rights reserved.
Plaid pattern on cover copyright © by danesteffes/iStockphoto. All rights reserved.

Library of Congress Cataloging-in-Publication Data
Partow, Donna.
  Making money from home / by Donna Partow.
    p. cm.
  "A Focus on the family book."
  Includes bibliographical references and index.
  ISBN 978-1-58997-608-5 (alk. paper)
  1. Home-based businesses. 2. Women-owned business enterprises. 3. New business enterprises.
4. Work and family. I. Title.
  HD62.38.P37 2010
  658'.0412—dc22

                          2009050041

ISBN: 978-1-58997-608-5

Printed in the United States of America

1 2 3 4 5 6 7 8 9 / 17 16 15 14 13 12 11 10

To Taraneh Joy

||||||||||||||

Contents

Part IV

Part V

Introduction

I haven't met you, but I suspect I already know two things about you:

1. You need to make extra money from home.
2. You need to make it starting *right now*.

Trust me, I get it. I've been right where you are. Granted, it was a long time ago, but the memory is vivid. I was at my desk in the investment-banking department on the twenty-eighth floor of a Philadelphia high-rise on Black Monday (October 19, 1987), the day of the largest stock-market crash in American history.[1] Not long afterward our entire department was eliminated. That was the end of any illusion I might have had about the stability of the American economy or the reliability of a company paycheck. It was also the beginning of my journey as a home-based businessperson.

Maybe your family has recently learned the same painful lessons. Or maybe you're being proactive by getting a side business going, just in case. Honestly, it doesn't really matter what prompted you to pick up this book. What matters is that you now have in your hands a step-by-step guide to making money at home in a global economy. And the time to start is now.

The Internet has changed the world forever. Take a quick visit to a Web site like oDesk, and you'll discover that computer-based work Americans charge $30 to $60 an hour or more for can be done by exceptionally well-educated, brilliant people in places like India and the Philippines for $2 an hour. You might not know anything about oDesk (or Elance or Guru), but I guarantee that every business owner or corporate executive worth anything sure knows about them.

The bad news is this: offshore competition. You can forget about the infamous medical transcription, work-from-home "jobs" that people still get suckered into. You can forget about any job or opportunity that doesn't require American ingenuity. Those jobs have gone, are going, or will soon go overseas. If you don't believe me, pick up your phone to make an airline reservation or to get technical support for your computer. Chances are, the person on the other end won't be living in America.

Now the good news: American ingenuity can't be outsourced. And you have it, whether you give yourself credit for it or not. Does a fish swim in water? If it's alive, I promise you, it's in water. If you're in America, you're swimming in American ingenuity all day, every day. I've now traveled on six continents and have discovered that no other country is like the United States. Although we've fallen behind in some areas, the independent entrepreneurial spirit that launched America in the first place is still what makes us unique in the world.

So here's what we're going to do together: We're going to give you a battle plan that begins with a comprehensive evaluation of just how much ingenuity you really have—all the way to the successful launch of your money-making enterprise. And if you already have a home business, I'll show you how to make it even more successful.

How To Use This Book

By purchasing this book, you've already taken the first step to establishing your own home business. In the following chapters you'll learn everything you need to know to plan and launch your business: how to choose a business that's right for you and your family, how to develop a business plan, time-management tips, marketing strategies, how to cut through legal red tape, how to lay a solid financial foundation, and much more. If you already have a business, you'll learn how to improve your bottom line and maximize your success. You may even find ideas for solving some problem that's been holding you back.

What you won't read in this book is a bunch of fluff or a relentless belaboring of the obvious. Instead, you'll learn everything you need to know to get started, *right now*, in a successful home business based on current technology. And because I recognize that technology changes daily, I've created a companion Web site for this book: www.making moneywithdonna.com. This site will continually update you on cutting-edge technology and opportunities. Throughout the book you'll find direct links for the latest information. You'll also find links to additional resources, as well as forms and charts designed to help you organize yourself, your business, and your household for success.

At the beginning of each section of this book, I'll be profiling the career of a woman who has succeeded at creating a home-based business. These women will add a fresh perspective and give you a look at the unique way each woman has made her business work. The profiled women may seem over-the-top, but each started small. Don't feel intimidated (or tired) when reading their stories. You don't have to take over the world; you may do as little or as much as you and your family feel is necessary for your business. However, if it is your intent to go big, this book will equip and inspire you.

Material featuring frequently updated topics is denoted with a ✳, and the URL (universal resource locator) for the Web page is noted as well.

At the end of each chapter, you'll find questions to help you clarify pertinent issues and discern the direction of your business. Some chapters also include assignments, enabling you to lay a business foundation in bite-size chunks. I highly recommend that you answer the questions and complete the forms as thoroughly as possible. The more work you do up front, the more likely your business will succeed.

Part I

Foundations for a Home-Based Business

Seven years ago, Kimber King was a busy stay-at-home mom with three boys, ages six, four, and two. She wasn't looking for a way to make money from home, but when she began using a line of products that dramatically impacted her health, she couldn't help telling everyone she knew about it. Kimber recalls, "The products were sold through a network marketing company and I actually had a very negative view of the industry. But the results I had with my own health far outweighed all the negative things I felt about the business." So she quickly signed up enough family and friends to reach the top rank level in her company in the first six weeks. Within ninety days, her monthly earnings matched the full-time income she had previously been paid in the corporate world.

Kimber soon began reaching beyond her immediate circle of contacts through social networking on the Internet. She recalls, "One night I stumbled upon a site on the Internet that described itself as a business-networking site. It was free and on the site you had the opportunity to create a profile page for yourself. I dove right in and started connecting with a ton of people. I did some things very naturally that literally launched my business on the Internet and to this day, from this one site I have an organization of six thousand plus members. Then I started branching out onto other sites like message boards and forums. I began cultivating online relationships mostly focusing on other stay-at-home moms."

> *Kimber also credits her parents for much of her success.*

Another of Kimber's success secrets is working with a personal business coach. Although she was earning a great income from home, she was working long hours on the computer and her income had remained the same for nearly two and a half years. "It was a very lucrative income for a stay-at-home mom of three," she says, "But I began to have great goals for my family and helping others, and I was frankly stuck."

Within eight weeks of working with the network marketing coach, Kimber was earning a monthly five-figure income and an annual six-figure income while reducing her workload to less than twenty hours per week.

Kimber also credits her parents for much of her success. "My dad instilled a spirit of excellence in me. By watching my mother work in her own hair salon, I learned how to treat customers." Kimber says the key is focusing on others. "It's always about them and not me! What are their needs? What are their goals? What are their strengths? What are their desires? It's never been about me and my income goals or rank advancements. If you focus on others, all that will come! One of my mentors says it like this: 'If you focus on the mission, you get the commission!' "

Trust in God is also central to her business approach. As she explains, "When I start a dialogue with someone, my main intention is to discover how I can bless them. It might not be about business at all. It's all about relationships first and then anything that flows out of it from there I leave up to God! I trust Him completely with my business and that He will also put those in front of me that I am supposed to serve. When people ask what I do to create success in my home business, I tell them two simple things: Pray and take action. I pray for those who are looking for me and for those I can serve. Then I pick up that phone or connect with someone. "Faith without works is dead!" I have faith in my heavenly Father to provide the way but I also know that I have to step out on that path in faith."

> *"When I start a dialogue with someone, my main intention is to discover how I can bless them."*

Kimber has stepped out in faith knowing that God is the provider in her home business and that's made all the difference. Now seven years later, she earns a six-figure income from home, working part-time, raising her sons, and modeling the same entrepreneurial spirit she saw in her own mother.

Discover the Advantages of Working from Home

Let me begin with a brief look at the "why" of running a home-based business to show you the benefits, because your motivation and belief in the benefits are what keep you going when the going gets tough. But then we'll quickly shift gears to the more essential and practical how-to suggestions on the following pages.

Like any job, working at home offers both advantages and disadvantages. In the days and months ahead, times of discouragement will come. You may struggle with prioritization and time management. In addition to those burdens, the physical and emotional demands of promoting your business can drain you. You may begin to wonder if all your hard work is worthwhile, and you may even be tempted to give up your plans. In those moments, turn back to this chapter, reexamine the many benefits of working at home, and redouble your efforts to succeed. Remember, anything worth having is worth fighting for.

Your Home Can Be the Center of Your Life

There's no place like home. I believe that with all my heart. Home can be the center of our lives, not just the place we come to recover from our lives. We can create an environment that fosters creativity and launch not just one narrow home business but a broad range of income-generating activities.

My first home-based business was in marketing communications: writing press releases, brochures, and ad campaigns. It was hard to get people to take me seriously as I tried to compete with the big-city advertising agencies. But I had a talent for writing and was absolutely determined to be a stay-at-home mother. I landed my largest client when I walked into his office wearing a dark pinstriped business suit and pushing my newborn in her stroller. This man said he was impressed with my motivation and touched by my priorities.

Remember, anything worth having is worth fighting for.

Over the past twenty years, I've launched countless different moneymaking enterprises. Some were dismal failures; others were wildly successful. Most were somewhere in between. As of this writing, I have a dozen income sources. Granted, some provide only $20 here and there. But hey, $20 is $20!

Let me illustrate. While away on a recent missions trip to Mozambique, I received checks from three businesses, totaling $800. The amazing part is that it was all passive income from businesses I had set up on autopilot on the Internet.

How would you like to earn $800 a week? Would you be thrilled with $800 a month? Maybe you plan to become a business tycoon and earn $800 a day. It's up to you! But whatever your financial goals, I'm here to tell you that anyone can make extra money or have a full-time career from home if he or she is willing to work smart.

For almost twenty years, I've been a leader in promoting home-based businesses for women. I have spoken around the country on the topic of women's entrepreneurship, including two events at the CIA Headquarters in Langley, Virginia, and three conferences hosted by Senator John McCain. I have loudly proclaimed my firm conviction that every man and woman in America should develop some creative way to make extra money from home. And, under appropriate learning conditions, children, too, should develop those skills.

You Can Be Available for Your Children and Others

By working from home, you can avoid the hassles and costs of day care (which are far more substantial than most people realize) and enjoy spending time with your children. Even if you have to hire a babysitter to watch your kids in your home while you work, you'll be available at a moment's notice if needed. And you can keep a watchful eye on all that goes on throughout the day rather than sitting at a desk wondering if your children are okay.

My older daughter, Leah, is now in college. She was homeschooled much of her life, and I was a stay-at-home mom throughout her entire childhood. Although I was often extremely busy working forty hours a week, and even more on my businesses, I was always available when she truly needed me. Won't it be nice, when your children reach adulthood, to look back and say the same?

Perhaps you have a disabled family member or are caring for elderly parents. Maybe someone in your home has a chronic illness, and you need to be available for doctor and other appointments. Working from home allows you to be there to care for them and gives you the flexibility to take time off during the day, setting your own schedule.

You Can Be a Positive Role Model for Your Children

Some would argue, "I'm too busy raising my children to run a home business."

I counter, "Don't you think it just makes sense to include your children in your business so they learn to be entrepreneurial and self-sufficient under God's sufficiency? Don't you think that training them to run their own businesses might prove to be more significant than running them around to various afterschool activities?"

Fortunately neither of my daughters has the mind-set that some corporation is going to give her a paycheck and job security for the rest of her life. That is an absolute delusion. We need to train our children for the real world, where wise people use the gifts God has given them to mind their own businesses—even if they also have careers. Both of my daughters, who are now nineteen and thirteen, have already had many moneymaking businesses. They've done everything from making bookmarks and jewelry to running my book table and processing credit-card orders from my Web site.

When my oldest daughter was fifteen, she organized a teen missions conference that attracted seven hundred people. I had very little involvement. How did she know how to do that? She's been working at Christian conferences since she was two years old! Leah has also raised thousands of dollars for her various missions trips by making and selling crystal bracelets.

In addition to being able to watch my children grow while I worked from home, they also watched me grow as a businesswoman. By observing me model entrepreneurship, both of my daughters learned valuable business skills.

You Can Help Shoulder the Financial Load

Not only can you work from home; you should. With few exceptions, it's unwise to rely solely on one income source in today's unstable economy. Now more than ever, I thank God that I have multiple streams of income from my various home-based enterprises. All over the world, mothers not only nurture their families, but they also play a vital role in ensuring the economic survival of their families. I've seen this with my own eyes as I've traveled worldwide—from the subsistence farmer in Africa bent over her crops with a baby slung on her back to the Asian mother selling items in the local market while children sit nearby, often working as well.

Women throughout history have contributed to the economic survival of their families. We can do the same, and if we exercise wisdom, we can do so in a way that won't detract from our role as nurturers. In fact, working from home will enhance all of the roles we play and increase our stature in the eyes of our family members. My children not only love me, but they also openly admire me. How can you put a price tag on that?

You Can Enjoy a Sense of Accomplishment

One of the most important things I hope my children have learned from observing me making money from home is that productive work is not a punishment; in fact, it's inherently rewarding. Many of us have experienced that exhilarating feeling of working hard to complete a project or the joy of beholding something we've made with our own hands. A home business will provide abundant opportunities for you to enjoy that exhilaration.

As the old saying goes, "If Mamma ain't happy, ain't nobody happy." It's equally true that when Mamma is happily enjoying a sense of accomplishment, everyone around her benefits. I think I've modeled a wonderful lifestyle for my daughters. It's a lifestyle I'm quite certain they'll choose to replicate.

You Can Be Your Own Boss

Many people fear dependence on a corporation because they have had the rug pulled out from under them or have seen it happen to so many of their colleagues. The days when you could rely on a company to look out for your best interests are long gone. While you're working diligently for XYZ Corporation, it's entirely possible they're filling out your pink slip. Once you establish your own home-based business, you'll have the pleasure of signing your own paycheck. And when you think you deserve a raise, you can give yourself one.

When you work for an employer, you're required to work when, where, and how *they* choose. When you have your own home business, you have more control over when, where, and how you work. Of course, you're still responsible to your customers, and there will be crunch times when you don't have a choice about how many hours you put in. But there is usually much more time flexibility when you are your own boss.

Once in a while when I'm struggling with some aspect of my home business, one of my relatives will joke, "Donna, you should go back to banking." But we all know I'm completely unemployable! I've been my own boss for too long, and I don't think I could ever go back to having someone else tell me what to do with my time.

You Can Continue Your Career

Many women spend years training for a career before their children arrive on the scene. Teachers, nurses, doctors, lawyers, and many other professionals can quite easily transfer their hard-earned skills to a home-based business. Knowing that your career isn't on hold will give you satisfaction, even though the majority of your time may be spent with family. This is especially important if you want to resume your before-children career after the children have grown.

> *The amazing thing about the Internet is how easy it now is for a woman to stay current and relevant in her field while mothering and earning money from home.*

The amazing thing about the Internet is how easy it now is for a woman to stay current and relevant in her field while mothering and earning money from home. These types of opportunities were hard to come by when I wrote my first home-based business book. Now they abound. Let's hear it for technology!

There Are Opportunities for Tremendous Success

When you work nine to five for someone else's company, to a large extent your boss controls how well you do. But when you work for yourself, only your ability and determination set the limits, assuming you start with a great product or service people want. Maybe there's something you've always dreamed of doing. Now is your chance to do it! You may aspire only to make a little extra money, but there's always the chance that your "silly idea" will catch on, and you'll find yourself transformed into a very successful entrepreneur. Someone has to think up those great ideas. Why not you?

I know a number of Christian women who earn six-figure incomes thanks to their home businesses. Yes, you read that right. Six figures! I even know women who've earned more than a million dollars, and one woman who has earned several million. With few exceptions, these women did not set out to achieve such tremendous success. They were just doing what they loved, and the success followed. Put another way, they were walking in obedience, and God's blessings chased them down the street and overtook them. It could happen to you!

The Top Ten Ways to Avoid Scams

1. **Surf with caution.** Understand that the mainstreaming of the Internet has created both good news and bad news for aspiring home-based business entrepreneurs. Good news: Opportunities abound. Bad news: Scams abound.

2. **Beware advertisements.** No legitimate company on the planet will ever advertise to hire an employee to work from home. Not gonna happen. Never. No, not ever. Why? Very simple: If a company had a legitimate interest in hiring employees to work from home, there would be an instantaneous pileup of current employees and their circles of influence. The very fact that a company is advertising work from home is your first clue that it's a scam.

3. **Never buy a list or directory of companies that supposedly hire people to work from home.** These are phony! Once and for all: The answer to the question of who will hire you, keep you secure, pay you lots of money, and grant you the freedom to set your own hours from home is *no one*. You don't need a list or directory of no one.

4. **Choose freedom or security.** I constantly hear from people who want the freedom of working from home as well as the perceived security of a job. Freedom and security are always

a trade. Will you give up some of your freedom for security? Or will you give up some of your security in return for freedom? You'll never have both in full measure. Accept reality: You cannot have your cake and eat it too.

5. **Understand the role of oDesk and similar outsourcing Web sites.** In the introduction, I mentioned the emergence of Web sites like oDesk and, in one sense, this is an example of companies looking for people to work from home. And yes, many Americans are trying to capitalize on this new trend. Some are even succeeding. However, for the most part, companies who post on oDesk aren't "hiring"; they're simply outsourcing on a project-by-project basis for the express purpose of not hiring employees. So although some opportunities exist, I believe sites like oDesk are actually bad news for any North American woman who wants to work from home and is hoping she might find someone to hire her. If you thought the competition was fierce when millions of Americans were looking to work from home, now millions more people around the globe are in the mix. You'll have to compete with people who are willing to work for a few dollars an hour, and it's nearly impossible to build a successful North American business like that. Now, if you're willing to move overseas, that's a whole new ball game, and oDesk can become your very best friend. That's well beyond the scope of this book, but if it's something you're interested in pursuing, read *The 4-Hour Work Week* by Timothy Ferriss.

6. **Know the code.** As soon as you hear phrases like "more work than I can handle" or "looking to train someone" or "just want to help others duplicate my success," run for the door. Or

click the mouse. It's a scam. If these people really had more work than they could handle, their relatives and friends would be beating down the door to get in on it. But since it's a scam and they've already driven away all their friends and relatives, they're on the Internet trying to scam you. Don't be fooled.

7. **Beware whirlwind friendships.** There are some unethical people whose entire marketing strategy consists of befriending people just to recruit them for this, that, or the other "business opportunity." Over the years a number of people have swept into my life with a friendship that felt more like a whirlwind romance. In every instance it turned out they were in a network marketing business. As soon as they discovered I wasn't interested, the whirlwind friendship ended, and they moved on to the next person.

8. **Check it out.** Don't rely on information provided by the person trying to sell you. Turn to Google, the Better Business Bureau, and the Federal Trade Commission (FTC) to verify the claims and promises.

9. **Take your time.** Don't let anyone pressure you into making a decision on the spot. If it's a great opportunity today, it will be a great opportunity a week from today.

10. **Big dollars should raise a big red flag.** It shouldn't cost more than $500 to $1,000 to launch a business from home.

Questions

1. What prompted you to pick up this book?

2. Why do you want to work from home?

3. What will motivate you to keep going when the going gets tough?

4. On a scale of one to ten, rate the following advantages of working from home:

    Your home can be the center of your life.   _____

    You can be available for your children and others. _____

    You can be a positive role model for your children. _____

    You can help shoulder the financial load.   _____

    You can enjoy a sense of accomplishment.   _____

    You can be your own boss.   _____

    You can continue your career.   _____

    There are opportunities for tremendous success.   _____

Pillars for Long-Term Success

You don't need a Harvard Business School degree or an MBA to prosper as an entrepreneur, but you do need to know and implement some keys to success. Understanding the following ten foundational pillars will help build the framework for your home-based business's longevity and profitability. Let's explore them now.

Shift Your Mind-Set from Consumption to Productivity

If you're going to become the wildly successful home-based business owner I know you can become, it is essential for you to get a new mind-set. Rather than viewing your home primarily as a place of relaxation and consumption, view it as a place of productivity. In other words . . .

- Home is a place to consume media in the form of radio and TV programs. But it could just as easily be a place where you create your own media (downloadable MP3s, YouTube videos, etc.) for others to consume.

- Home is a place to consume food, but you could just as easily produce food for sale. I have a friend who markets her brother's salsa recipe.
- Home is a place we consume books and magazine articles, but many people produce books and articles from home.
- Home is a place we consume the Internet in vast quantities of time, but thousands are producing content designed to market their information or products via the Internet.
- Home is a place we store our consumer goods, such as clothes and jewelry, but we could just as easily produce an eBay business to sell clothes and jewelry from home.
- Home is a place we store junk, but we could just as easily sell our junk at yard sales and flea markets. When we run out, we can go buy other people's junk and resell it at twice the price we paid. (Don't laugh. I know a woman who does exactly that and does so quite successfully.)

It's a very simple mind-set shift: from viewing home strictly as a place to consume what others have produced to viewing home as a place where you can produce products and/or information to market to others for their consumption.

Now you're thinking like an entrepreneur, and you'll begin to see opportunities everywhere.

Choose a Business You Really Enjoy

Time and time again, home businesses fail because the proprietor selected an endeavor for all the wrong reasons: "The woman down the street is selling beauty products, and I can too." Never mind that you've never worn makeup in your life and have zero interest in the beauty industry; there's money to be made, and you intend to make it. That, my friend, is a formula for disaster.

Choose a business you can pour your heart into, something you can believe in and feel good about. That's why chapter 5, on choosing the right business for you, is so vital. The more closely you and your new business match, the more successful you'll be. You'll enjoy your business more and will be less prone to burnout.

Do a New Kind of Homework

Every truly successful home-based businesswoman I know did thorough research before launching out on her own. Most have also taken courses on some aspect of running a business. These women took advantage of the free counseling and training services available to them through the Small Business Administration (SBA), local university extension services, and similar nonprofit organizations.

> *Every truly successful home-based businesswoman I know did thorough research before launching out on her own.*

So start there, but then be willing to go to the next level and invest in your own business development. Don't be afraid to exchange your time and money for business education. In particular, you probably need training in technology and marketing. Go to live seminars. Enroll in Internet teleseminars. The Internet contains a vast storehouse of information. Read up on your line of business and find out how other people in similar circumstances have succeeded. Fill your iPod or MP3 player with business training and personal motivational teaching. If you're going to succeed at working from home, become a full-time student of business success. (For further suggestions on entrepreneurship training, visit www.makingmoneywithdonna.com /training.✳)

Become a Specialist

Imagine this: You've just discovered you have a brain tumor, and the only cure is a delicate surgical procedure. The doctor turns to you and says, "Actually, I'm a podiatrist, but I feel like I can do pretty much any- thing. Hand me the scalpel." What would you do? You'd run for the door, that's what!

Once upon a time a doctor was a doctor was a doctor. But this is the age of the specialist. People want to deal with the expert in the field. Yet so many home-business owners set themselves up as generalists. It'll never work. When you're flying solo, the power lies in focusing your energies. What one thing gets you out of bed in the morning? What one thing are you eminently qualified to do? Focus every ounce of your energy right there and forget everything else. If you do, you'll become an expert in your field, and business will come to you.

That doesn't mean you can't have multiple streams of income, but all of your business enterprises should be related to your central area of expertise. In other words, don't be both a hairstylist and a dog groomer. Be a beauty consultant who does hair, makeup, nails, facials, and personal shopping while selling skin-care and nail-care products and accessories. See the difference?

Be Persistent

Your business isn't going to succeed overnight. However, if you believe your endeavor is worthwhile and you really want to work from home, planning and persistence are all that remain. In time you'll reap the harvest, but first you must plant the seeds! Don't be content with the current crop of clients, or your business will soon dry up.

Be willing to invest the time and energy required to continually cultivate future business. Send out flyers to people who have never used your product or service before, and send thank-you notes to those who have. Maintain an e-list of previous and prospective customers and routinely send them helpful information just to keep your name fresh in their minds. A monthly e-zine is now a business essential for everyone.

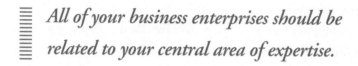 *All of your business enterprises should be related to your central area of expertise.*

Persistence plays a particularly important role in getting started. You may run into obstacles and resistance, and you may be tempted to give up. Building a business can be emotionally and physically tiring. The difference between those who fail and those who succeed often comes down to one more knock on the proverbial door.

View your home business as a way of life, not a particular product or service. When one idea flops, pick another and run with it. How many times? As many times as it takes. Simply put, success means getting up one more time than you fall down!

Discipline Yourself

There's no doubt that self-discipline is critical for success. To some it comes naturally, while others have to work at it. Of course, the degree of self-discipline required varies according to circumstances. A mother of five who works forty hours a week requires more self-discipline than an empty nester working twenty hours. Establish accountability with your spouse, business partner, or friend, and determine deadlines and checkpoints for progress.

If discipline is a weakness, join an online mastermind group that will challenge you to set goals and then hold you accountable for achieving them. You might be asking yourself, "What is a mastermind group?" The concept is credited to Andrew Carnegie, the wealthy steel-industry tycoon, who used mastermind groups to build his success.[1] A mastermind group is two or more people who put their heads together to generate ideas and tap into resources to achieve a particular goal. Actually, King Solomon long ago declared that "two are better than one" (Ecclesiastes 4:9)! Find a person or two or three, set some goals (either individual or joint), then encourage and hold one another accountable to achieve them. To locate a group that will suit your objectives, I invite you to visit www.making moneywithdonna.com/mastermind ✻ for current recommendations.

Present a Professional Image

Your image is an extremely important part of your business. Although it's hard to define precisely what is meant by "professional," there are a number of factors that can work together to ensure that you make a favorable impression on your associates and clients:

- Your appearance. What you wear while working around the house is no one's business but your own. However, if you want to set an atmosphere that promotes work, you may find that getting dressed is more conducive than your old bathrobe and fuzzy slippers. When you do come in contact with the public, be sure to present the image appropriate to your industry and clientele.
- Your Internet presence. Few things are worse than an obviously amateur Web site. Either have one professionally done (which should cost no more than $500) or forget it and create a blog

instead (more on how to do that later). Web 2.0 technology has leveled the playing field, so you can have and do anything a multimillion-dollar corporation can do. In fact, there are some things you can do even better. Just be sure to use cutting-edge Internet tools and technology. (See www.myhome madebusiness.com/internet-tools/. ❋)

- Your marketing material. Later we'll devote several chapters to marketing, but for now, keep in mind that professionally printed materials are an absolute must if you're going to convey a professional image.

Build a Solid Support System

Over and over again, the women interviewed for this book said one of the pillars that undergirded their success was a supportive spouse, family, and friends. Unfortunately this is something you have little control over—but you can exert some influence. Long before you put up the Open for Business sign, work to win the enthusiastic support of your family and friends. Sell them on your ideas and assure them you are serious about your endeavor.

> *Long before you put up the Open for Business sign, work to win the enthusiastic support of your family and friends.*

Once things are under way, you can head off potential conflicts by clarifying expectations. If you were a full-time homemaker prior to going into business, you may have taken your child's forgotten book to school or dropped off a report at your spouse's office. Make it clear that you remain willing to help in a crisis, but by and large, your family shouldn't expect you to do all the things you once did as a full-time homemaker. (Balance this with grace and mercy, of course!)

If you're moving from full-time outside employment to a home-based business, make sure your family understands that you're still working—just in a different place. In other words, if you worked at a downtown office from nine to five, would your daughter expect you to drop everything to bring lunch money to school? Of course not. Be careful here, or you can end up with the worst of both worlds: the pressures of a working mother and none of the slack usually afforded to her.

> *Make it clear that you remain willing to help in a crisis, but by and large, your family shouldn't expect you to do all the things you once did as a full-time homemaker.*

Friends may also have expectations you'll no longer be able to fulfill. Perhaps you used to make five dozen brownies from scratch for PTA meetings. Let them know they'll have to settle for purchased cookies or find another refreshment volunteer. Maybe a special friend is in the habit of dropping in unannounced during the day. She needs to know that you're unavailable for socializing during work hours. All of this should be done with tact, of course, so feelings aren't hurt and friendships aren't damaged.

On the positive side, you can enlist the aid of your friends. Just recently a close friend called and said, "Donna, I know you hate details, and I'm great at them. Here's what I'm thinking . . ." She then proposed taking over a particular aspect of my home business and agreed to accept a percentage of any additional income generated thanks to her organizational initiative. That's a win-win for both of us.

Market Yourself and Your Business with Confidence

You are the sales and marketing staff. Even if it doesn't come naturally to you, you must learn to market yourself and your business without apology. When you exude confidence in your skills and services, your customers and clients will be reassured as well. Likewise, if you're unsure about what you have to offer, others are likely to detect this and have the same misgivings.

Just today I exchanged e-mails with a woman who is coaching me toward greater business success. I've recognized that I don't place enough value on the gifts God has given me or the decades of effort I've invested developing my expertise. As a result I'm inclined to give away resources I should be charging for and tend to undercharge even when I do charge. Cultivate self-confidence by being worth what you charge and charging what you're worth.

> *Don't take it personally when someone chooses not to do business with you.*

One very practical thing every woman who wants to start making money from home should do is avail herself of informative, positive, uplifting teaching via CDs, the Internet, podcasts, and other forms of media. You get the idea. Listen and learn as you drive around, take your daily walk, or even do household chores. Constantly strive to learn and grow so you'll have solid reasons to feel confident. (For some of my favorite informative and uplifting resources, visit www.makingmoney withdonna.com/uplift/. ✱)

Learn to Deal Effectively with Others

Your business will inevitably bring you into contact with many new people, including customers, subcontractors, and vendors. Your ability to deal effectively with them will directly affect your success. Consider becoming a student of human behavior by taking personal-development courses. More important, each morning you should pray over the day's events, the people you are scheduled to meet, and the unexpected interruptions that will occur. Don't take it personally when someone chooses not to do business with you, especially if that person is a friend or family member. Keep it all in perspective. Ask God to give you wisdom and grace as you deal with each person and situation.

Recap: Ten Pillars for Home-Based Business Success

1. Shift your mind-set from consumption to productivity.
2. Choose a business you really enjoy.
3. Do a new kind of homework.
4. Become a specialist.
5. Be persistent.
6. Discipline yourself.
7. Present a professional image.
8. Build a solid support system.
9. Market yourself and your business with confidence.
10. Learn to deal effectively with others.

Questions ||||||||||||||||||||||||||||||||||||||||||||||||||||||||||||||||||||||||||||||||||||||||||||||

1. Do you have a consumption-oriented mind-set? If so, how can you make the shift to a productivity-oriented mind-set?

2. In what areas of your life might a shift from a consumption mind-set to a productivity mind-set yield a business opportunity?

3. What type of business might you enjoy?

4. In what area can you picture yourself as a specialist?

5. Compared to others you know, how persistent are you? What can you do to develop this quality?

6. How self-disciplined are you? How can you become more so?

7. What kind of image do you usually present (e.g., casual, professional, disorganized, sloppy, etc.)? What do you think you'll find most challenging about image and presentation in a business?

8. Who might be part of your support system? When can you make contact with each of these people?

9. What marketing strengths do you already possess?

10. How can you develop your marketing skills? What local and Internet-based training opportunities can you investigate in the coming weeks?

11. What are your strengths and weaknesses in terms of dealing effectively with others?

12. How can you build on your strengths and minimize your weaknesses?

Your Home Office

If you haven't already done so, it's time to set up a home office. You'll need one even if you're just trying to figure out what type of business you want to have. An office is a nonnegotiable, but it doesn't have to be large.

Believe it or not, my first home office was a closet. Not a walk-in closet. It was a tiny hall closet in a one-bedroom apartment, and it was just wide enough to hold a three-foot desk and barely long enough for me to squeeze into a chair behind the desk. As long as I didn't want to move at all, I was okay. But you know what? I was incredibly efficient in that office. I went in there only when I was serious about working, and when I was in there, I remained serious about working—unlike goofing off for hours a day in the large office I have now. Just writing these words, I'm tempted to go move into a closet somewhere in the house.

The Elements of a Practical Home Office

Your home office must be a dedicated space, both for tax purposes and for your own sanity. Do not even think about having it at your kitchen table. Find a place that can be exclusively devoted to working on your home business. Whenever possible, find a way to close up shop each day. If you can shut a door, fine. If not, hang a curtain or a piece of fabric over the entrance. Put up a partition or a decorative screen. Do something that enables you to physically and mentally walk away when the day is done.

Look around your house with fresh eyes: any possibilities in the basement, attic, garage, or back porch? Could a trip to Home Depot or Lowe's and some sweat equity work wonders? If you take your business seriously, your family and friends will be more inclined to respect your efforts.

I would caution you against setting your office up in the corner of your bedroom. I briefly made that mistake, but it didn't take long to realize why this is inadvisable. There is neither rest nor romance when you look up from your pillow and catch sight of the pile of unfinished tasks out of the corner of your eye.

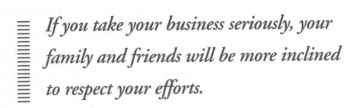

If you take your business seriously, your family and friends will be more inclined to respect your efforts.

Search flea markets or yard sales to set up the basics of an office: a table and chair, a calculator, a pencil cup, a stapler, paper clips, desk trays, and so on. (A friend of mine bought a beautiful desk for $7.50 at an auction!)

The best way to keep organized is to create a place for everything. It sounds hackneyed, but it really is much easier to keep things in place that way. Strive for a professional appearance.

Color

You should give careful attention to which colors you select for your office. Research demonstrates that colors actually have a physical effect on the human body. Red, for example, increases blood pressure and is associated with energy and stimulation. So if you need a boost to get going, buy some red curtains, a red wall hanging, or whatever. Yellow is a bright, cheerful color, so you may want splashes of yellow in your work area—a dried flower arrangement or a tablecloth, for example. If you tend to be hyperactive and your work requires a relaxed frame of mind, blue and green are associated with reduced blood pressure, relaxation, and tranquillity. My walls are light green.

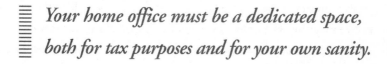

Your home office must be a dedicated space, both for tax purposes and for your own sanity.

Avoid blacks, browns, grays, and earth tones. These are associated not only with fatigue and sedate behavior but actually make the available space seem smaller as well. White, on the other hand, is a neutral color that increases the perception of space. It's hard to go wrong with white or off-white walls.

By the way, any money you spend fixing up your office is completely tax-deductible. Take your start-up budget and splurge on a gallon of paint at Wal-Mart. It'll do wonders for your frame of mind, and I promise you'll get a great ROI (return on investment) for your time and money.

Computer

A computer with fast Internet access is an absolute must for any home-based business. Have a yard sale and sell some of your junk, if you need to, in order to buy one. Do keep in mind, however, that few things will kill your productivity like surfing the Internet, and it can quickly become addictive. I speak from experience! Predetermine set times to check your e-mail and social-networking sites and limit the amount of time you allow yourself to wander about in cyberspace. Otherwise, you can sit in your home office all day, away from your family, yet achieve nothing for your family. Now that's the worst of both worlds, and your goal is the best.

Purchase a printer with a scanner/copier/FAX. Having it all in one machine is amazing—the best bang for your cyber buck.

Phone

In the perfect world, you will have a separate business landline *and* a cell phone that is for business only. If you can't afford to do that, you'll have to prioritize your business needs. Perhaps a cell phone is secondary to a great computer because the majority of your work will be done via e-mail. There are some great bundles out there for phone services—be a wise shopper.

I praise handless cell phone devices such as a Bluetooth. Some states require them if you plan on talking while driving. I don't recommend this practice however, especially when kids are in the car. Now talking while doing the dishes or chopping veggies is a different story, but I still don't recommend making business phone calls this way. Do chat away with a Bluetooth while finding babysitters and for social calls. The handless devices make multitasking so much simpler and efficient.

Desk

You'll be spending many hours at your desk, so it pays to invest some thought and planning into making it right from the start. Purchase the most comfortable desk and chair you can afford. Consider ergonomics or you may wind up with aches and pains. You have enough things wearing you down without having to endure back and neck strain from working in an uncomfortable position. Your increased efficiency will pay for the desk (and chair) several times over.

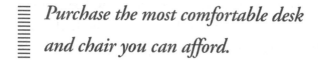

> *Purchase the most comfortable desk and chair you can afford.*

As with your office in general, avoid clutter on your desk. As a rule of thumb, if you don't use an item at least once a day, it doesn't belong on top of your desk. Staplers, tape dispensers, and the like are wonderful gadgets, but if all they do is occupy space, let them be wonderful in a drawer.

Organize a Filing System

As a general rule, try to throw away more than you file; otherwise you'll drown in a sea of paper. Save only what you really need. For example, don't save an entire magazine; save only the article of interest to you. Of course, some things will certainly need to be saved for retrieval at a later time.

A good way to set up your initial files is by labeling a series of file folders A-Miscellaneous through Z-Miscellaneous. That way, you can create specific subject files as warranted. For instance, once your G-Miscellaneous file has accumulated five letters from George's Paper Supply, you can make a subject file especially for this company.

Another approach is to set up temporary files by marking folders in pencil or by attaching a removable Post-it label. Affix a typed label only when you are certain you need a file for that particular subject. It doesn't make sense to make a separate file for every piece of paper you want to keep. If you do, you'll have one hundred files within a few weeks.

Eventually you should have a file (by company or individual name) for every major customer or vendor you do business with. You should also make subject files for special projects you're working on or topics that relate to your business. For example, you may be developing a new product. Make a special file and put everything pertaining to it in one place (regardless of who the vendor is). Or you may hope to write a book on child rearing someday. If you come across helpful articles from

The Top Ten Most Useful Office Supplies

Each office has unique requirements, which will become self-evident as time passes. Don't rush out and spend a fortune on unnecessary supplies. Start with only the basics and build your inventory in the months ahead. The following list of commonly needed office supplies will serve as a guide:

- Desk organizer
- Drawer organizer
- Postage meter
- File folders, hanging files, and labels
- File folder storage, even if it's just a plastic bin
- Three-hole punch
- Desk trays
- Stapler and staples
- Three-ring binders
- Printer

time to time, file them all in one subject folder rather than by author or some other means.

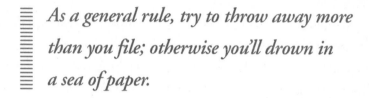

As a general rule, try to throw away more than you file; otherwise you'll drown in a sea of paper.

File folders and labels are both available in a wide variety of colors, so you may consider color-coding your system. For example, vendors may be in yellow folders, clients in blue folders, projects in green folders, and so on. Alternatively, you may opt to use all manila folders with different colored labels.

Set Specific Working Hours

One great advantage of working at home is the power to set your own hours. Unfortunately, it can also become a real problem. Some people don't work enough hours. Others work too many. It's essential for you to remain well balanced in all of this, or one of two things will happen: Either you'll work too few hours and lose your business or you'll work too many hours and burnout yourself or your family.

If you're married, first sit down with your spouse and hammer out a specific work schedule (see chapter 16). Then gather the children to discuss your proposal and ask for their input and support. Once you've established specific working hours, post them at the entrance of your home office. If you have young children, it might be fun to allow them to create and/or decorate your Working Hours sign and help you post it on the door. Do not allow yourself to go into your office during nonworking hours unless you have a compelling reason. For the record, checking your e-mail for the hundredth time does not constitute a compelling reason.

Your business may involve going out in the evenings for sales meetings and such. You may not be able to predict which night of the week people will agree to meet with you, but you can set boundaries. For example, you work only two nights per week. Or you never meet with potential clients on Wednesday night because that's reserved for family. At the same time, you should set goals for how many nights per week you will go out on sales calls. If two weeks go by and you've not had any meetings, your family should feel free to say, "Hey, didn't you commit to working on Tuesday and Thursday nights? What's up?"

Do not allow yourself to go into your office during nonworking hours unless you have a compelling reason.

One final thought: As a general rule, I don't recommend seeing clients in your home. Meet with them either at their office or in neutral territory such as at a coffee shop. The exception might be if you're involved with a direct-selling or network-marketing business, and you're inviting only people you know personally or those who are friends of trusted friends. Still, caution is advised. Your home should be used primarily for handling the at-home aspects of your business to preserve the peace and privacy of your household.

Create a Brain-Nourishing Environment

"I have no idea what business to start. I have no idea what new products I should offer. I have no idea how to grow my business." Ever hear yourself mutter those sentences? The fact is, to succeed in a home business, you need a constant stream of great ideas. Where do they come from? It's not all serendipity. You can actually create a "brain-nourishing" environment that breeds great ideas. Following are some tips to get you started:

1. Remember, the factory of the information age is the human mind. You don't need employees or expensive equipment to succeed in business today. You do need to tap into both your right brain (creative, divergent thinking) and left brain (analytical, convergent thinking). Set a kitchen clock for ten minutes and throw out ideas (no matter how outlandish) rapid-fire (right-brain activity). Then spend twenty minutes analyzing them (left-brain activity).

2. The best ideas start with a passion to solve a specific problem or to find an answer to a burning question. Simply asking yourself the right questions is a launching pad. The world changed forever when the first nomad stopped asking, "How do we get to water?" and asked instead, "How can we get the water to come to us?"

3. If you want to generate great ideas, "ready, fire, aim" should be your motto. Yes, I know it sounds backward, but here's what I mean. First, clearly identify the problem by asking the right questions (Ready). Next, throw out dozens—even hundreds—of possible solutions, from wacky to wonderful, from silly to sublime (Fire). Last, identify one of these ideas that appears to have the most potential. Refine it and give it your best shot (Aim).

4. Newspapers, magazines, and books are filled with idea fodder. So is nature. Children are infinitely creative and can often spark new ideas. When Edwin Land took a picture of his young daughter, she asked, "Why can't we see the picture now?"[1] That question inspired Land to invent the Polaroid Land camera.

5. Most ideas come when you're not trying too hard. Many come in the middle of the night. The trick is to write them down immediately so they aren't lost. Stock notebooks and microcassette recorders wherever your best ideas usually strike: by your bedside, in the car, in the bathroom.

6. Break mental blocks. If you're bogged down in a problem and need a boost, begin scribbling with a pencil or pick up a small object with your nondominant hand. The unfamiliar muscular movements from the subordinate side of your body will trigger an electrical flow in the nondominant side of your brain. The net result? New connections, a new perspective—possibly a new idea.

7. Whether you have a fleeting notion or a product concept you just can't shake, you'll never know whether it's a great idea or a fluke . . . until you put it out for all the world to see. A fair idea put to use is much better than a great idea kept on the polishing wheel. Remember: It won't fly if you don't try!

The Top Ten Idea-Generating Moments

According to research conducted by Charles "Chic" Thompson, author of *What a Great Idea,*[2] the top ten idea-generating moments are when you are

1. Sitting on the toilet
2. Showering or shaving
3. Commuting to work
4. Falling asleep or waking up
5. In a boring meeting
6. Reading at leisure
7. Exercising
8. Waking in the middle of the night
9. Listening to a church sermon
10. Performing manual labor

8. Don't re-create the same dull, stark environment that has stifled corporate creativity for years. Replace fluorescent lights with halogen, incandescent, or natural light. Play uplifting classical or jazz music. Sit by the window and daydream! Have a large whiteboard and markers for mapping out projects. Fill your office with flowers, plants, books, stimulating artwork, decorator accents, maybe even a hammock. Make it a place you *want* to spend time! I love spending time in my home office; my family might say I love it too much! Each morning, after breakfast and morning devotions, I pour myself a mug of hot lemon water and then head up to my office. When I report to work, the first thing I do is light some scented candles and then turn on quiet praise music, and I'm ready to generate some great ideas.

Questions

1. Where will you set up your office?

2. List the equipment you'll need to get started, and ideas for obtaining it.

_____   _____

_____   _____

_____   _____

_____   _____

_____   _____

_____   _____

3. Note your office hours for each day. (Why not make a large Mom Working sign and post it on your office door? Begin holding office hours today!)

Monday

Tuesday

Wednesday

Thursday

Friday

Saturday

4. List the office supplies you'll need. Begin to purchase them, one by one if necessary.

_____	_____
_____	_____
_____	_____
_____	_____
_____	_____
_____	_____
_____	_____
_____	_____
_____	_____

Assignment

1. Purchase your supplies and equipment.
2. Set up your filing system.

Your Business Plan

You've probably heard the saying "Failing to plan is planning to fail." Nowhere is this truer than in business. Before you can even determine which business is right for you, the first step is to create a business plan.

Yes. You heard me. *Before* you choose a line of business. Even if you don't need a loan. Even if you don't even know how much money you want to make. The process of starting a business plan will help you focus your goals and eliminate options that will not fit your plan. Then you'll refine your business plan at each step. This process will keep you in a position to evaluate if your business is succeeding or failing and which aspects of your business need to change over time.

Please don't make the mistake of relying on intuition or vague, unwritten objectives. Get your plan in writing. You should be able to summarize in thirty seconds exactly what you're in business to do. If you can't do that, you're not ready to launch yet. Focus!

I want the principles outlined in this chapter to be in your mind during the selection process for your business.

An important part of being taken seriously is taking yourself and your business seriously. So be sure to take the extra time to produce a plan that is thorough, accurate, and neat. If you plan to remain a one-person operation forever, it need not be more than a couple of pages.

Nevertheless, it's a vital document that indicates to you and all interested parties (your family, financial institutions, and insurance agencies) where you plan to go and how you intend to get there.

> *You've probably heard the saying "Failing to plan is planning to fail." Nowhere is this truer than in business.*

Be precise and knowledgeable about every aspect of your business. Know your products, customers, and competition. You can't afford to wing it. Have your spouse or a friend ask you tough questions about your venture. This chapter outlines the components of a business plan and even includes a Business Plan Worksheet.

Write the Vision and Make It Plain

You do not have to be a talented writer to write a business plan. Of course you want it to be professional, but this is not an essay competition. What you want to do is write the vision and make it plain. The very act of writing forces you to be specific, rather than vague. A woman with a meaningful specific plan will beat a woman pursuing a wandering generality any day of the week. Be specific. Know where you want to go. You may not get there, but at least you'll know where you're heading.

Develop a Unique Selling Proposition

What sets you apart? What makes you or your business truly different from everyone and everything else out there? The same God who creates every snowflake to be completely unique will empower you to create a completely unique business. He has already poured uniqueness into your appearance, personality, gifting, and life experience. Talk to people who know you best. Ask them what's truly unique about you. Remember: As a solo entrepreneur, you are the business so lend your own style to create a personal brand. (One helpful resource worth checking out is *The Brand Called You* by Peter Montoya [McGraw-Hill, 2008].)

Create a Vivid Description of Your Potential Customer

One of the biggest mistakes new business owners make is believing the whole world is your potential customer. Even as I was writing this book, I went through a phase during which I tried to convince myself that "Surely men need to start a home business too." I proceeded to go through the book trying to "de-mom-ify" it and make it more generic.

Wrong. Wrong. Wrong. My potential customers are not fifty-year-old single men. My potential customers are women of faith, most of them married with children still at home. By narrowing my focus, my likelihood of success doesn't diminish. Quite the opposite. Many business experts recommend posting a picture of your typical customer directly above your desk. You can clip this from a magazine or download from the Internet. Let it be a constant visual reminder of whom you are targeting.

Include a Thorough Analysis of Your Competition

Who are your competitors? If you will only operate locally (although I don't advise it), a quick search of the local Yellow Pages is still a good start. But for most businesses, the competition is on the Internet. So fire up a search engine and get to work. Find out what people are saying, both pro and con. Evaluate their pricing, product line, Web presence, marketing strategy, etc. What are they doing that you need to emulate? How can you do it better? With tools like Twitter and Facebook, you can develop a generic customer survey. So if you are starting a book club, ask people what they like/dislike about book clubs they've joined in the past, what they would like to experience through a club, etc. The Internet is a great gift—open it up!

Include a Strategy that Allows for a Reasonable Amount of Risk

One of the services I provide is Home Business Success Coaching via the Internet. Women have to complete an application process in order to become part of my training program. One of the questions is "How much money do you want to make per month?" and another is "How much money are you prepared to invest to launch your business from home?" I had to chuckle at one application received today: She would like to earn $4,000 per month and is willing to invest "$50 or less" to get started.

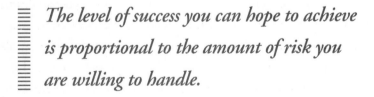

The level of success you can hope to achieve is proportional to the amount of risk you are willing to handle.

That's not reality, friends. You must be willing to assume a reasonable amount of risk. Your business is not guaranteed to succeed. In fact, you'll probably have plenty of so-called failures along the way. I've certainly fallen on my face more times than I care to number. It's not a failure if you learn from the experience.

One thing I urge all of my coaching clients to do is watch the movie *The Pursuit of Happyness* before launching a home business. You should watch it and pay attention to two things. First, the business that seemed like a complete failure actually prepared Chris Gardner for his ultimate success. He learned to persevere when everything looked hopeless and how to face rejection with a gracious smile. He learned how to face defeat, day after day, and still get up and try again. Second, notice how much he risked and the sacrifices he made.

It's time to trot out an old cliché: Nothing ventured, nothing gained. You must risk your money and time. You must risk failure and rejection. Watch that movie over and over again until you become inspired because without that level of intense determination, you'll never succeed. And the level of success you can hope to achieve is proportional to the amount of risk you are willing to handle.

Invite Input from a Broad Range of People with Various Backgrounds

It's amazing how powerful asking good questions can prove. So ask people for feedback on your proposed business, then keep quiet and listen. You can ask your mom and your best friend for input about your suitability for a particular business, but when it comes to hammering out the details of making it work, it's time to bring in a broader range of viewpoints. There's a time to turn to experts and now is that time. Fortunately, there is an amazing amount of support available through your local Small Business Administration advisers. Also investigate their affiliated program, the Service Corps of Retired Executives (SCORE). Many home-business owners have received priceless insight from these retirees. SCORE's slogan is "Counselors to America's Small Business" and as we know, there is wisdom in the counsel of many. Make an appointment today.

Find a Numbers-Cruncher Person to Review Your Budget

Many entrepreneurs are visionaries and big-picture people. That's certainly the case with me. So you need to connect with someone who is good with details and can help you evaluate how realistic your proposed budget is. Here again, SCORE volunteers can provide invaluable help.

Put Most of Your Effort into the Marketing Plan Portion

Without customers, you don't have a business, and so a great marketing plan is essential. Throughout parts III and IV of this book, you'll learn both traditional and Internet marketing strategies you can incorporate into your plan. Become a student of marketing. It can actually be fun experimenting with different approaches to discover what works best. Just remember to celebrate the marketing victories and quickly recover from the marketing bombs. You can definitely plan on experiencing some of each.

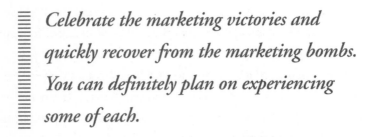

Celebrate the marketing victories and quickly recover from the marketing bombs. You can definitely plan on experiencing some of each.

Take Your Plan Seriously

Your business plan is not just an exercise to be completed so you can cross it off your checklist of things to do to get started. If you do it right, it will become your roadmap to success. So invest thought, time, and prayer into the preparation process. Then refer to it on a regular basis. You might even want to mark your calendar to review your plan once a month to evaluate your progress.

At the same time, you have to be willing to adapt if you realize your initial plans were unrealistic. That's the beauty of computers—documents are easily changed. I'm old enough to remember typewriters, so don't complain that keeping your business plan up-to-date is too difficult.

Two Final Thoughts

If you plan to succeed, you need more than a good business plan. You need God's blessings. I believe there are two things you absolutely must do in order for your business to experience God's favor. First, be sure to tithe. I usually give God the first fruits by tithing on my entire income (before expenses are deducted). You might feel more comfortable offering a tithe of your actual income (after expenses are deducted). That's something you'll have to pray about. But whether gross or net income, tithing is not an option for the Christian business owner. God tells us to put Him to the test on this and see what happens when we honor Him with the fruit of our labor.

Second, if you are married, plan to honor your husband's boundaries regarding your business. When you are developing your plan, ask him how much time and money he is willing to see you invest. Then operate within that framework. If your husband says, "I'll support your home business as long as you don't work more than four hours per day" and you honor his request, I'm absolutely convinced you'll generate more profit in those four hours than you would if you defied your husband and worked eight hours. I would go so far as to say that anything you earn in defiance of your husband is ill-gotten gain and is not under God's protection. Strong words? I know! But I've been at this for twenty years and have learned many lessons, most of them the hard way.

So take it from me: Honor God and your husband (if you have one) and your business will go so much better than it would in the absence of honor.

Buſineſſ Plan Workſheet

As you continue reading this book, the answers to each of these questions will emerge, so consider your business plan a document-in-progress at this point. For now, leave blank any questions you aren't sure about. You should turn here again and again as you move closer to starting a home-based business. You can find this worksheet at the end of the chapter and also as a PDF file at www.makingmoneywithdonna/business _plan/.

Queſtionſ |||||||||||||||||||||||||||||||||||||||||||||||||||||||||||||||||||||||||||||||||||||||||||||||||||||||||||||

1. When do you want to have your business plan completed?

2. Do you know people or organizations who can help you develop your business plan? List their names and areas of expertise:

Assignments ||||||||||||||||||||||||||||||||||||||||||||||||||||||||||||||||||||||||||||||||||||||||

1. List ten possible names for your business. Now begin to narrow
    the list down until you find the right one. Check to make sure
    the name is not already a trademark of someone else. (Warn-
    ing: This might take a lot longer than you think. Be sure to get
    opinions from family and friends as well.)

    _____   _____

    _____   _____

    _____   _____

    _____   _____

    _____   _____

2. Check on zoning laws, if warranted.
3. Open a post office box, if desired.
4. Register your name with the city or county clerk.
5. Apply for applicable licenses or permits.
6. Talk to your insurance agent.
7. Open a business bank account.
8. Complete your projected budget.

Business Plan Worksheet

1. Describe the business in detail.

   _____

   _____

   _____

   _____

   Company Name: _____

   Address: _____

   Owner: _____

   Legal Structure: _____

   (Attach copies of legal documents to your business plan.)

2. State the major goals and objectives of the business:

   _____

   _____

   _____

   _____

3. Discuss the special skills and experiences you bring to the company. Describe your qualifications. (Attach a résumé to your business plan.)

   _____

   _____

   _____

4. Describe the products or services offered.

   _____

   _____

   _____

5. What advantages do your products or services have over those already on the market?

_____

_____

_____

6. Describe your market (those people most likely to buy your product or service).

_____

_____

_____

7. List current customers, if any.

_____

_____

_____

8. Indicate when, where, and how you plan to advertise and publicize your business.

_____

_____

_____

9. List all equipment and supplies you will require to get started.

_____   _____

_____   _____

_____   _____

_____   _____

10. Attach a copy of your first-year budget. (See the next section for tips.)

First-Year Operating Budget

(Note: You will need to extend this budget out to twelve months using a spreadsheet or financial software.)

	January Budget	Actual
1. Cash on hand (start of month)	_____	_____
2. Cash received	_____	_____
3. Total cash available (Total 1 and 2)	_____	_____
4. Disbursements		
a. Office supplies	_____	_____
b. Postage	_____	_____
c. Telephone	_____	_____
d. Car, travel	_____	_____
e. Entertainment	_____	_____
f. Advertising/promotion	_____	_____
g. Accounting, legal fees	_____	_____
h.Insurance	_____	_____
i. Utilities	_____	_____
j. Taxes and depreciation	_____	_____
k. Interest	_____	_____
l. Loan payment	_____	_____
m. Payroll	_____	_____
n. Other (specify):	_____	_____
	_____	_____
	_____	_____
	_____	_____
Total cash paid out	_____	_____
5. Cash position (Total line 3 minus total line 4)	_____	_____

Part II

Exploring Your Options

Tamera Aragon took a bold leap of faith and quit her high-paying, high-stress corporate position in April of 2003 to work from home as a full-time real-estate investor. Beginning with almost nothing but prayer and determination, Tamera has bought and sold more than 175 houses and has purchased more than $10 million in real estate all over the United States.

Because Tamera's true passion is helping others get the most out of life, she immediately began sharing her real-estate investing strategies. "So many people asked me for the secret to my success. Just for efficiency's sake, I began posting my strategies, tools, and resources on the Internet." Eventually Tamera created seventeen unique Web sites, each addressing different aspects of real-estate investment and entrepreneurship. She gradually learned how to package her information into marketable electronic products, including e-books and teleseminars. One of her most popular items is her e-book *Avoid Foreclosure.*

Following the ſmart-ſtepſ Plan

The business closest to Tamera's heart these days is her mentoring service, Coaching U2 Profits, through which she has already personally trained 120 real-estate investors. "I just put together this formal program two years ago, and it absolutely took off. It's a combination of online group classes, coursework (downloaded off the Internet), telephone coaching, and real-world assignments. I feel like I've finally found exactly what I was created to do. I love investing, but I love investing my life building investors even more!"

From day one Tamera approached her business like a professional. She converted a guest bedroom into an office, with a new desk, computer, fax machine, and all the office supplies needed to get started in first-class style. She established a separate phone number for her business so she could answer it in a more professional manner than her personal line. Now she uses an 800 number to make it easier for her customers to get in touch.

She set working hours and has stuck to them faithfully. Tamera put up a piece of paper on her door that reads "Mom's at work. Do not disturb. I love you. Thank you for understanding." She adds, "If the door's shut, my family is not allowed to knock unless the house is burning down." Tamera also relies heavily on her calendar, where she marks off family and personal time. "At some point I have to walk out and shut the door, because I love what I do and could easily work all day, every day. That's not fair to my family." She admits, "In the beginning I was working way too many hours. They almost had to drag me out of there."

Real-estate investing is a complex industry, so Tamera relies on what she calls her "power team." It includes a legal service, an insurance agent, a title-and-escrow company, a contractor who oversees all remodels for fixer-uppers, home inspectors, and a team of five property managers in different parts of the country to keep an eye on the condition of the various properties she owns. Tamera obviously works with real-estate agents and lenders as well. She has a bookkeeper, who manages her twenty-nine mortgage payments each month, and a CPA for more complex issues and tax advice.

In addition to her power team, Tamera has both a traditional personal assistant and a team of virtual assistants. The traditional assistant manages the out-of-home office (shared with her husband, also a business owner), where Tamera goes to occasionally meet with clients and industry professionals, but the assistant also comes to her home office as needed.

> *Tamera put up a piece of paper on her door that reads "Mom's at work. Do not disturb. I love you. Thank you for understanding."*

Tamera uses low-cost virtual assistants for the most mundane of tasks. She explains, "Today you can hire someone in another country who will work much cheaper. I could easily waste all day just reading e-mail, but reading e-mail doesn't generate income. Instead I pay someone $2 to sort out the junk e-mail while I focus my energy on developing deals that yield thousands of dollars in profit." She believes e-mail management is extremely important; otherwise you can be in your home office all day but get little accomplished.

Other tasks she has delegated to virtual assistants include fielding incoming phone calls in response to promotional campaigns using a script and even making phone calls to prospective customers using leads, lists, and a script. Tamera began delegating after reading *The Power of*

Focus.[1] "Many women struggle with the idea of paying someone else, thinking, *If I have to pay someone, won't that mean I make less money?* Actually, the opposite is true. I gave away the business tasks that require more time than I had and those I just don't like or am not skilled at doing. That frees me up to focus on those aspects of my business I actually enjoy. And that makes me more productive and more profitable."

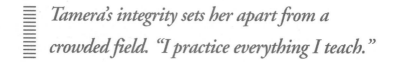

Tamera's integrity sets her apart from a crowded field. "I practice everything I teach."

To get started, Tamera wrote down all the tasks she did each day. Then she began, one by one, delegating routine jobs and projects that drained her energy. "It's not easy to give up control," she explains, "but your business isn't going to grow if you don't give up pieces of it. There are only so many hours in the day."

Tamera does have one other secret to her success. "Once my daughter was in school all day, I started struggling with loneliness." So she bought a lapdog to keep her company—a three-pound Yorkie named Chloe. "It may sound silly, but anything that adds to your happiness adds to your ultimate success."

And this is one home-based businesswoman who has certainly experienced ultimate success. Her combination of professionalism and generosity has earned her an outstanding reputation in the field of real-estate investing and has won the attention of many of America's top real-estate investment experts. She notes, "Anyone can put up a Web site declaring herself a real-estate investment adviser, but eventually people figure out who is the real deal and who isn't." Tamera's integrity sets her apart from a crowded field. "I practice everything I teach. Everything I advise others to do is something I have done myself and had success doing." So take the advice you've just read and put it to work for you!

What Home-Based Business Is Right for You?

Establishing any business requires both time and money. Before taking another step forward, sit down and honestly evaluate how much of each you're willing and able to invest. This will determine, in large measure, the nature of the business you should undertake. As a general rule, it takes at least $500 to $1,000 to get a business off the ground. I earned that much at my last yard sale. Whatever it takes, get the funds you need to give your business a fighting chance to thrive. I'll give you some ideas about how to do that in the next four chapters.

Like anything else in life, starting a home-based business is a matter of trade-offs. Just remember: You will get out of your business whatever you're willing to put into it. No more and no less. Do you envision yourself as a world-renowned entrepreneur? Wonderful. Be prepared to pay the price. On the other hand, maybe you simply need to earn $100 per week to supplement the family income. That's great, even though you'll never be among the rich and famous. The important thing is to be clear about your priorities.

By far, the most important decision you have to make is what type of business to launch. Remember, this is a personal matter, and what's right for someone else isn't necessarily right for you. Don't make the mistake of leaping into an arena that may be totally unsuitable for you just because opportunities exist. Whether or not you already know exactly what you want to do, and even if you've already launched a business from home, please take time to carefully work through the exercises in this chapter.

Consider Your Education, Training, and Career Experience

List your educational background, beginning with kindergarten. What do you know about yourself because of your school experiences? Don't limit it to "I'm good at math." For example, I walked out on high school biology when it came time to dissect a frog and told the teacher I'd rather receive a D (even though I was a straight-A student) than participate in something I found repulsive. I learned that I make decisions with my heart, not my head. This type of information is important to know.

If you dropped out of school, what does that tell you about yourself? If you won awards or preferred extracurricular activities, what does that say? Look for clues that might lead to your success. Have you had any special training, such as first aid, horseback riding, public speaking, self-defense, or CPR? If you've had more than a day's worth of training, list it. If you paid to learn it and enjoyed the experience, could you learn enough to teach others who'd be willing to pay you to be the trainer?

List every job or money making business you've ever had, beginning with your lemonade stand. Under each item, list every skill required and acquired, along with every lesson learned, including what each job taught you about yourself. My lemonade stand taught me I work better with a deadline. I was always having lemonade and comic-book sales, but when the carnival came to town, I went into overdrive and made a bundle of money. Why? Because I knew it was in town for a limited time. That sense of urgency motivated me. It still does! What motivates you?

Look to Your Personal Interests

List five things you enjoy doing with your free time. Might any of those be developed into an income-generating activity? Look over your book collection. What category do most of them fall into? What topic have you read widely on? What section of the bookstore or library do you gravitate toward? Have you learned enough to teach others, whether through writing, speaking, or a combination of the two?

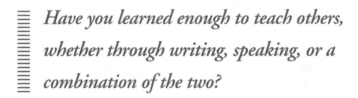

Have you learned enough to teach others, whether through writing, speaking, or a combination of the two?

What Web sites do you frequently visit? Could you build a Web site or create a blog of your own offering similar information? I love surfing political Web sites and do it even though I'm not getting paid. I could quite easily develop a blog that provides links to my favorite political stories each day. (I'll show you in chapters 12 and 14 how to make money with a similar strategy. For now, you're just finding out which business would be right for you.)

If you could talk only about one topic all day every day for the rest of your life, what would it be? What excites you? What energizes you? What topic comes up in conversation that you can't stop talking about? Trust me: If you'll make that topic the heart of your home business, you're guaranteed to succeed.

List any special talents you have, from the obvious, like music, to the not-so-obvious, like your talent for putting people at ease. Do you golf or play tennis? Are you good enough to give lessons? You get the idea.

Evaluate Your Normal Activities

Write out a detailed description of your typical day. Don't skip anything! You're looking for the usual, the routine.

Is there anything on the list you absolutely love doing and would do all day even if no one paid you? Maybe you love holding babies. Or ironing. Maybe you love surfing the Internet. I don't care what it is, there's a way to turn it into a business!

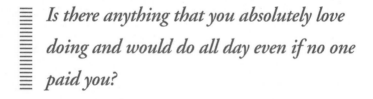

Is there anything that you absolutely love doing and would do all day even if no one paid you?

Is there anything you absolutely detest doing? Do you think other people detest it too? Housecleaning is the perfect example. So start a housecleaning referral service, where you get paid a fee to schedule and manage reliable housecleaners.

Next, create a two-column list. The first column should be labeled *Task* and the other *Skills Required*. Now, carefully evaluate the tasks you do each week and the skills required for their successful completion. Don't overlook things like driving kids around. I know a woman who started her own afterschool shuttle service! Do you iron? Lots of people who wear professional clothing (uniforms, suits, or dress shirts) would love to have someone iron for them and are willing to pay, especially if you pick up and deliver.

Evaluate Your Unusual Activities, Interests, and Life Experiences

What is unusual about you? Would others be fascinated by it? Were you raised in the jungles of South America, with monkeys and boa constrictors for pets? Did you backpack through the Middle East by yourself for two years? Do you collect spiders or grow flowers indoors in the winter? People are fascinated by the offbeat and unlikely. How can you capitalize on that fact?

The Top Ten Socioeconomic Trends

As you ponder your personal inventory, also ponder the top socioeconomic trends in North America (and much of the world) today.[1] If you can merge who you are with what's happening in the world, you've got a one-two punch.

1. Aging baby boomers
2. Migration to smaller, sunnier destinations
3. Universal connectivity (e.g., cell phones, wireless Internet)
4. Economic globalization (increased competition from overseas)
5. Increase in self-employment
6. Living off the grid—solar, wind, hydroelectric, geothermal, and wireless technologies are creating a new breed of pioneers
7. Increasing physical and property security needs
8. Education for youth and adults
9. Exploding health-care industry
10. Luxuries as necessities

For example, one of my friends grew up in the jungle because his parents were missionaries with New Tribes Mission. His first business was selling paintings of tribal scenes he recalled from his youth. Today he runs a videography business, but many of his customers are missions organizations who recognize that his unique upbringing and understanding of tribal culture enable him to bridge the gap between the people they're reaching on the field and those they're reaching out to for funds.

Consider Problems You've Solved

If you hope to succeed in a home business, you must become the kind of person who walks, talks, eats, and breathes the subject around which you're building the business. So look closely at problems you've personally solved and obstacles you've overcome. For example, if you've struggled all your life with poor health or battled weight control and found solutions, look no further for the focus of your business. I don't care how shy you are; if you've found a real solution to a real problem, your concern for other people alone will empower you to share it. Sharing is just another word for selling. And don't kid yourself: If you're going to stay in business, you absolutely must learn to sell.

Brainstorm challenges you've faced that have forced you to search for answers—answers you can market to others for a profit. Use the following list as a jumping-off point to brainstorm marketable solutions for common problems:

- Personal
- Physical (weight loss, medical)
- Spiritual
- Mental
- Emotional
- Family relationships (spouse, parents, children, family of origin, extended family)

- Work relationships
- Marriage
- Parenting
- Financial
- Money management
- Debt reduction
- Savings/investing
- Cost cutting
- Income generation
- Decisions on big-ticket items
- Events in the seasons of life (pregnancy, childbirth, childrearing, sending kids to college, wedding planning, retirement)
- Illness
- Death of loved ones

As you brainstorm the problems you've personally encountered in any or all of the above areas, reflect on any type of gadget or system you created that others might want to use. For example, a former neighbor of mine thought grocery-cart seats were too dirty to place her child in, so she sewed a cloth cart seat to shield her child from the germs and to make for a more comfortable ride. I urged her to market it as a product. She didn't . . . but someone else must have, because I've seen them in shopping carts.

In addition, study the list above and then listen to people around you and what they're saying about problems they're facing. Something that came easily to you might be a struggle for others. If you can help solve their problems, they'll help you build a profitable home business.

What Business Do Your Friends and Family Think Is Right for You?

There's such a thing as false modesty. Some people have amazing talents but refuse to give themselves any credit. Are you one of them? Consider the compliments you receive. Do people compliment you on how well you dress? Become a fashion consultant. Are people amazed at your ability to stretch a dollar? Write an e-book filled with your best strategies and market it via the Internet.

> *Something that came easily to you might be a struggle for others. If you can help solve their problems, they'll help you build a profitable home business.*

Make it a point in the coming weeks and months to notice what people compliment you on. Then ask yourself—and you might even ask them—if there's a business opportunity in there somewhere. Would people pay you to help them become as good as you are at this skill or activity?

Along the same lines, ask at least five people who know you well to complete the "Third-Party Analysis" that follows. (You can photocopy it from the book or send them the following link so they can download it off my Web site, www.makingmoneywithdonna.com/third-party-analysis. ✳)

Questions

1. What's the most important thing you learned about yourself and your potential business based on your education, training, and career experience?

2. What's the most important thing you learned about yourself and your potential business based on your personal interests?

3. What's the most important thing you learned about yourself and your potential business based on your unusual interests, activities, and life experiences?

4. What's the most important thing you learned about yourself and your potential business based on specific problems you've solved?

5. What's the most important thing you learned about yourself and your potential business based on compliments you often receive?

6. What's the most important thing you learned about yourself and your potential business based on the feedback obtained through the Third-Party Analysis?

7. What's the most important thing you learned about yourself and your potential business based on your review of the Top Ten Socioeconomic Trends?

Assignment |||||||||||||||||||||||||||||||||||||||||||||||||||||||||||||||||||||||||||||||||||||||||||||||||

Ask at least five friends to fill out the following Third-Party Analysis

Third-Party Analysis

Complete the following exercise, evaluating the skills and interests of your friend or spouse. The information will be most helpful if you're as honest as possible.

1. List five things she seems to enjoy doing with her free time.

2. List any hobbies or talents she has that may be marketable.

3. List any technical or unique skills she possesses.

4. List five things other people say she is good at.

5. How supportive will her friends and family be of her business venture?

6. How much time do you think she could devote to a home-based business? Per day _____ Per week _____

7. Based on your answers to these questions, list five possible home-based businesses that might be suitable for her.

Global Electronic
Flea Markets

Now we get to the fun part: exploring ways to make money. The advent of the Internet has given us more opportunities than ever to make money from just about anywhere. This is a big advantage for entrepreneurs. Let's start by looking at global electronic flea markets for two purposes: first, earning some quick cash to pay for business startup costs; second, as an ongoing revenue source.

Open your eyes. Look around. If you're an American, I guarantee you're surrounded by stuff. Right now, that stuff just causes clutter, collects dust, and creates more work for you. But blink and open your eyes again. This time, look at all that stuff with price tags on it. You can sell all your stuff to someone else and let it clutter up someone else's house, collecting dust and creating more work *for them* rather than you.

Go through your house room by room, cabinet by cabinet, closet by closet, drawer by drawer. No item is too big or too small to consider selling. If you can imagine life without it, sell it. Your life will be exponentially better with less clutter and more cash in the bank. (You'll find a lot more help and a step-by-step strategy for transforming your home with my book *Becoming the Woman God Wants Me to Be.*)

Meanwhile, go through your clothes, books, CDs, DVDs, toys, kitchen gadgets, you name it. If you have two when one will do, sell the extra. If you're married, have your spouse and your kids do the same. In this economy, everyone is looking for a deal. You can do them a favor

---

The Top Ten Garage/Yard-Sale Tips

1. **Promote your event.** Put an ad on craigslist and in the local newspaper. Post flyers in local stores and community bulletin boards. Put out large, sturdy, easy-to-read signs the morning of your sale, with arrows pointing the way to your house. Good signs are a must. Remember to take them down after the sale.

2. **Clean everything and present your items with pride.** If people see dirty or broken junk on any of your tables, they'll quickly walk away, assuming you're a person who doesn't take proper care of your things.

3. **Price everything in advance using removable labels.** Rule of thumb: Price items one-third of original value, but be prepared to negotiate.

4. **Place the most appealing big-ticket items near the curb to motivate people to stop and take a closer look at everything.** If you have guy stuff, put that near the curb as well. It will make it easier for wives to convince their husbands to pull over for a look-see!

5. **Create a department-store-like environment.** Organize items by category: toys, tools, kitchen, home decor, jewelry, clothes. Clean and display items with care. Put books on a shelf, hang clothes on a rack, and so forth. Presentation counts!

6. **Appoint a dedicated cashier.** Set up a small table, close to the house, where the money guy (or gal) will be stationed.

while improving the quality of life for yourself and your family. All that excess stuff is your ticket to money in your pocket. Plus, getting rid of it will declutter your home, making it easier to clean and simplifying your life. It's a win-win-win situation.

Have enough $1 and $5 bills, as well as quarters available to create change. Go to the bank two days ahead to obtain at least two $10 bills, four $5 bills, twenty-five $1 bills, one $10 roll of quarters, and $5 in nickels and dimes. Never, ever walk away from the cash stash. If no one will help as your cashier, wear a fanny pack. You'll need a calculator and plenty of grocery-store plastic bags.

7. **Have an extension cord available so people can test electrically powered items.** (If it doesn't work, you should throw it out. Please don't try to sell broken merchandise to some trusting person. If an item is broken but may be worth something for parts or is an antique, mark clearly that it is being sold "as is.")

8. **Grab bags.** Put a bunch of similar, small items (screws, nails, tiny toys, hair ties, etc.) into clear Ziploc bags and price them at $1, $2, or $5 rather than dealing with nickels and dimes.

9. **Sell food and beverages.** A pot of hot water with instant coffee, hot cocoa mix, and tea bags can generate some extra cash. In warmer weather, have a cooler with water and soda pop. Lemonade and iced tea are also popular. Be sure you have cups, napkins, and other supplies. A bake sale doesn't have to be home-baked goods (although that's more profitable). You can purchase products at the grocery store the night before and make a nice markup.

10. **Soft background music is a nice touch.**

Now, take everything that's too large to ship and every item worth less than $10 and sell it at a yard sale. That will provide the seed money for your online resale business. (See the following "Top Ten Garage/Yard Sale Tips" sidebar.)

Welcome to the Online Global Flea Market

Once you've completed your yard sale (don't donate your leftover stuff to the Salvation Army yet), you are now in a position to determine if you want to graduate to selling on eBay and similar sites. Now you can forget the hassle of your yard sale and join the world's biggest online flea market! Thousands of people buy and sell on eBay every day—even people who aren't computer whizzes. These online stores are so easy to operate that my daughter Taraneh set up one for herself in less than an hour—when she was ten years old!

Selling products at these global flea markets is one of the few ways to launch a home business with almost no up-front investment. You can start with virtually no money and build a million-dollar business. All you need is a computer, a digital camera, and stuff. Most of us already have that. If not, use the money from your yard sale to help you get started.

Introducing eBay

The hardest part of starting any business is finding customers. When it comes to most Internet-based businesses, the biggest challenge is driving traffic to your Web site. You can set up shop on the Internet, but if no one knows where you are, it's pretty difficult to make money. Enter eBay! You don't have to attract potential customers. The potential customers are already there, just waiting for you to show up with products to sell. It's the difference between opening a store in an empty cornfield in the middle of nowhere and opening up in a bustling mall filled with people. There's more competition in the mall, but there are also plenty of customers to compete for.

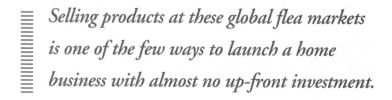

Selling products at these global flea markets is one of the few ways to launch a home business with almost no up-front investment.

As of this writing, eBay is by far the most popular spot on the Internet for buying and selling. Perhaps that's why there are currently more than 88 million registered users buying and selling on eBay, generating more than one million sales per day.[1] You can become one of them.

Most people casually surfing around the Internet are looking for information. Or hanging out on Facebook looking for interaction. They aren't looking to buy something and often don't appreciate feeling like they're being "sold." But with eBay, people are there specifically to buy. That makes your job of selling to them infinitely easier.

Sellers and Buyers on eBay

There are two players involved in every eBay transaction: the seller and the buyer. You, the seller, will pay a fee to set up your auction, you'll list the starting bid and a reserve price (the secret price you won't go below), and you'll announce in advance when the bidding will stop. Auctions can run one, three, five, seven, or ten days. Most experts agree that seven days is typically your best bet. Keep in mind that the lower you start the bidding, the more bidders you'll attract.

The buyer (or bidder) hunts for great deals or a promising auction and then bids against others to secure the item at a great price. The trick is that bidders typically don't know until the last second who won and what the final price was. Within the category of buyers/bidders, you have two very different types of people: collectors and bargain hunters. That's not to say collectors don't like bargains, but that isn't their primary motivation. A collector is someone with a passion, and typically that person will pay a bit more if you have something the collector is absolutely determined to own. So think about whom you want to do business with and plan accordingly.

The Basics of Buying and Selling on eBay

With eBay, users must enter their name, address, telephone number, and credit card number to begin bidding and selling products. You'll also have to pay a small fee for each ad you post. As a general rule, you should list items worth more than $10 each to justify the advertising expense. Insertion fees, as they're called, currently range from $0.10 to $4.00, depending on two things: the minimum bid and the reserve price, if you set one. In addition to insertion fees, some big-ticket items, such as real estate or automobiles, have larger fees attached. (To verify the most recent fee structure, visit http://pages.ebay.com/help/sell/insertion-fee.html. ✸)

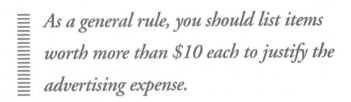

As a general rule, you should list items worth more than $10 each to justify the advertising expense.

In addition to the insertion fee, which you pay whether or not your item sells, eBay collects a final value fee—a commission based on the actual selling price of your item. You can estimate fees in advance, using special calculators like the one at New Life Auctions (www.newlife auctions.com/calc.html) or doing an Internet search for "eBay calculator."

Getting ſtarted on eBay

Here's a step-by-step battle plan for getting started on eBay (these principles apply to all electronic flea markets):

1. Create your eBay user ID and password. Just click your way to www.ebay.com to get started.

2. Check out "My eBay Page." This is where you keep track of all your activity and communicate with buyers and other sellers via the message center. There are also helpful notification programs on eBay that provide daily status reports on your various listings as well as let you know what has and hasn't sold, when your buyer has submitted payment, and so on.

3. Familiarize yourself with the "My Seller" account summary. This shows you how much you're earning and what it's costing you (in eBay fees).

4. Set up a clever "About Me" page. Post a photo of yourself and your cat if you're specializing in cat supplies. Make it unique! If your computer has the capability, be sure to add audio (and I'm sure video will be available by the time this book is in print). You can link your "About Me" page to your Web site, and vice versa.

5. Make the most of online learning tools. It's no secret what it takes to succeed on eBay. The company has a vested interest in your success, so it's gone out of its way to provide the tools you need. On eBay's "Sell" page, you'll find a "How to Sell" video tutorial that will walk you through the entire selling process. You'll also find several sections devoted to various aspects of selling:

- Determining an item's value
- How to set prices

- Creating your own eBay store
- Setting up an auction
- What's selling well now
- Shipping rules and regulations

One of those resources is advice from fellow eBay sellers, most of whom are more than willing to answer questions. Just turn to eBay's discussion boards for feedback from experienced sellers. Be absolutely certain you know and follow eBay regulations. Otherwise, eBay will suspend your account rather swiftly, and you'll be out of the game. Be sure to check out "eBay University Learning Center," eBay's selling basics online training program (http://pages.ebay.com/help/sell/selling-basics.html). E-Bay also offers classes at locations around the country. Another popular resource is TurboLister, a free online tool that makes it easier to post professional-looking eBay lists. (See http://pages.ebay.com/turbo_lister.)

6. Set up a PayPal account. PayPal is the standard medium of exchange on eBay. It's free and easy to open an account. Just visit the Pay-Pal site (www.paypal.com). Once you cross the threshold from casual user to business owner, you'll need a merchant account to accept credit cards as well. PayPal now offers those services for a reasonable monthly and per-transaction fee.

Start Making eBay Money from Your Extra Stuff

Now gather up all the items worth $10 or more that you didn't sell at your yard sale and post them for sale on eBay or whatever online flea market you've chosen. After you've sold all of your own trash and treasures online, it's time to venture forth into your neighborhood, volunteering to help family and friends empty out their attics, garages, and storage units in return for the opportunity to sell their stuff. Even if they want to keep a percentage of the proceeds, you risk nothing. You pay them only if you get paid. They win because the junk is out of their house and in yours.

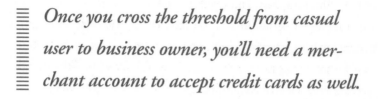

Once you cross the threshold from casual user to business owner, you'll need a merchant account to accept credit cards as well.

Follow the same procedure you used with your own stuff: If it's worth less than $10, sell it at a yard sale and use those funds to invest in your business. Items over $10 should be photographed, cataloged, and posted for sale online.

Finding Stuff to Sell on eBay at Garage and Yard Sales

Once you've exhausted the resources of family, friends, and neighbors, move on to yard sales in your community. Shop for bargains on the weekend. Remember, you're looking only for items you can sell online for more than $10 and that you can purchase for a fraction of the price you plan to ask on eBay. Photograph, catalog, and put the items on the Internet on Monday for twice (or ten times) the price you paid. If you accumulate enough unsold items, have another yard sale or give the unsold items to the Salvation Army and take the tax deduction.

Start Making More eBay Money

Once you've started generating income by selling used stuff, it's time for you to determine if you want to take your online global market business to the next level. I recommend this line of income because it's a low-to-moderate financial investment, it's fairly safe, and once the setup is done, the income is passive, meaning that your time investment per transaction is low and that leaves you with more time for family or ministry. And, as you'll see later, your product sales on eBay can overlap with other types of businesses, each of them cross promoting the other.

If you decide to get serious, then there are some pieces of equipment you'll want to buy. You need a decent computer with high-speed Internet access and a reliable printer stocked with ink. A regulation postage

---

The Six Best Places to Look for Yard-Sale Items

A note of caution: You can get in big trouble if you resell a recalled item. See U.S. Consumer Product Safety Commission (www.cpsc.gov/cpscpub/prerel/prerel.html) for a list of recalled items. Check especially baby products and toys! You certainly don't want to pass along a danger to an unsuspecting buyer.

- **Kitchen.** Look for small appliances you never use, extra dishes, pots, pans, and silverware. Even old spices and unused pantry items.
- **Bathroom.** Look for toiletries, makeup you don't use, extra towels, or washcloths. Even cleaning supplies you don't like or won't use.
- **Bedroom.** Most Americans own way too many clothes. Chances are, you need only a fraction of the clothes now cluttering up your closet. Simplify. If you haven't worn it in a year, sell it. Sort through shoes, hats, gloves, jewelry, linens, and room decor. Everything. Get rid of the clutter and turn it into cash.
- **Kids' bedrooms and playroom.** Our family's two biggest moneymakers were clothes from our teenager's room and

scale for determining shipping costs is another must. You might also upgrade your digital camera. Great pictures are probably the most important element of running a successful eBay business. People want to see what they're buying, and they want to see it from a variety of angles.

Develop a Specialty

The more successful online sellers develop a niche or a type of product to specialize in. You don't need more than a dozen products for sale to

old toys that my twelve-year-old hadn't bothered with in years. There's big money to be made selling all your kids' junk. It will also make it much easier for them to keep their rooms clean when there's less stuff to mess up the place. Sell those old stuffed animals, toys, dolls, action figures, comic books, coloring books, old crayons and markers, games, and so on. Let your kids keep some money from the sale of their stuff.

- **Basement, yard, attic, and other storage areas.** Empty these out! Be brutal now. It's in storage because you don't need it and don't use it. Sell it and get something you do need: extra cash.

- **Other people's yard sales.** This might sound crazy, but you can make lots of money by buying low and selling high. The week before your yard sale, go to other people's yard sales and snap up bargains. Buy from them for a nickel and sell it a week later for $0.50 or even $1. My neighbor, a single mom, does this and supports herself and her four children in style, selling other people's yard-sale stuff at her yard sales for a profit.

make money on eBay. Return to chapter 5, "What Home-Based Business Is Right for You?" Choose a subject you feel passionately about and begin selling related products. Become an expert so you'll know what's popular and how to price items correctly. Also, as we'll see in later chapters, you can attract business to your eBay store by blogging, writing articles, and networking socially on sites related to your chosen area. People like to buy from knowledgeable people. The more you demonstrate your expertise to buyers, the more likely they'll want to do business with you.

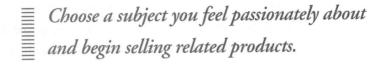

> *Choose a subject you feel passionately about and begin selling related products.*

Be Smart with Pricing

Don't just randomly guess what you think an item might be worth. The only question is this: What are people willing to pay? An item might be worth a million dollars in your mind, but if you overprice it, it isn't worth a dime. Overprice items, and you won't be in business for long; underprice, and you're running a charity, not a business. Price items right by doing your homework. Check the prices of products at major retailers, both online and off, because shoppers today do the same kind of research before they decide to buy from anyone. You can subscribe to eBay's Marketplace Research (http://pages.ebay.com/marketplace _research/) to learn how much products have sold for and how many times they had to be relisted before they sold or the auction closed.

Understand Keywords

Remember that the majority of eBay bidders find what they're looking for by using the search function. Be sure to use carefully chosen and accurate keywords in your title and description (eBay gives you fifty-five characters in your headline). Be sure to use all of them. This will help you get hits. Important keywords include the brand, color, size, and model number of the item you want to sell.

Create an Efficient System

As your Internet resale or online auction business grows, you'll need to set up routines and standard operating procedures. Keep notes as you go along so you can track what works and what doesn't. You can also identify simple steps that can be delegated to other family members so you can focus on the more complex aspects of your business (acquiring and pricing products, for example). You may have to invest some money to increase your effectiveness. For example, eBay sells various templates and business-management resources on the "Seller Tools" page (http://pages.ebay.com/sell/tools.html). As your Internet business grows, it just makes sense to reinvest in it so it can grow even more. That's basic business practice.

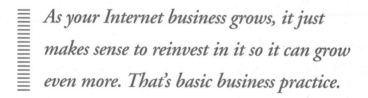

As your Internet business grows, it just makes sense to reinvest in it so it can grow even more. That's basic business practice.

You'll also need to manage inventory so you don't run out of stock. This has been one of the greatest challenges for me—finding that balance between overstocking inventory (which isn't cost effective) and understocking (which results in unhappy customers). It's more art than science, but be alert to the fact that you need to remain profitable in the short term by keeping inventory at a minimum, while remaining profitable in the long term by delivering what and when you promise so your store has a great reputation. It's not easy!

You should have a standard routine you follow each day for checking e-mail, checking your eBay account, processing and packaging orders, and then taking them to the post office or calling a pickup service. Although it may cost more to have UPS come to your house, you have to consider what your time is worth and whether standing in line is the best use of your time.

Going Wholesale

If you have decided that Internet sales is the way to go, you'll want to keep your Internet resale business growing, and so you'll need a steady supply of products to sell. You can stick with a routine of spending Friday and Saturday visiting local estate, yard, and rummage sales, and then photographing, pricing, and posting these one-of-a-kind items for sale on Monday. That's cost effective but extremely labor intensive. Individually researching and pricing unique items every week can be time consuming and mentally draining.

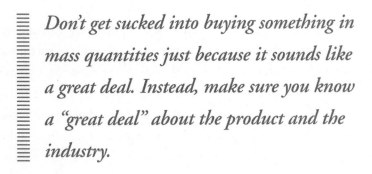

Don't get sucked into buying something in mass quantities just because it sounds like a great deal. Instead, make sure you know a "great deal" about the product and the industry.

Eventually your time might be better invested in purchasing many-of-a-kind items for resale. Although you'll have to spend more money up front, you'll save time and earn more money in the long run. To do so, simply search online for wholesalers to find potential suppliers of new merchandise in your niche. *A word of warning:* Resist the temptation to buy ten thousand of any single item. That's how people lose money with an eBay business and end up back at the local flea market, trying to off-load cartons of unsold items.

You'll need a resale license (aka state sales-tax ID number) to do business with wholesalers. In most states these are issued free of charge, although some states now charge a reasonable fee, which is typically less than $25.

Multiply Your Earnings with Dutch Auctions

You can improve your efficiency and profitability on eBay by hosting Dutch auctions—an auction with multiple winners. So rather than running one hundred identical auctions for one hundred items, you host one auction for one product but *award one hundred winners.* On the downside, you typically earn less per item with a Dutch auction than you do with individually auctioned items. Part of that is because you lose the element of scarcity that typically drives up prices. There's always a trade-off.

Wholesale on eBay Stores

If hosting eBay auctions sounds tedious, you might prefer setting up a more traditional eBay store, and then market your items solely through the Buy It Now (BIN) function. BIN is becoming increasingly popular on eBay because some people don't want to spend time bidding at auctions, only to walk away with nothing. The site also has its own version of an online mall called eBay Express. You might check out those options as well.

Stick with What You Know

Don't get sucked into buying something in mass quantities just because it sounds like a great deal. Instead, make sure you know a "great deal" about the product and the industry. Remember, you're building your wholesale eBay business around your passion, not around whatever product happens to be on sale. Stick with what you know and then hunt for bargains. Don't hunt for bargains only to find out what you didn't know; namely, that no one wants to buy it, and that's why you were able to buy fifty thousand for a bargain!

Clothing, accessories, electronics, household goods, toys, and sporting goods are some of the hottest sellers on eBay. It can be very hard to source these products new from the distributors. But many eBay sellers make excellent profits buying these products from liquidation and surplus dealers. One of the largest and easiest to deal with is Liquidation.com. They use an auction format similar to eBay. *One word of caution:* Check the shipping charges before bidding.

Warehouse Stores

Another strategy is shopping for wholesale deals at warehouse stores like Costco and Sam's Club, and then reselling at a markup. In particular, these stores have sensational deals on seasonal items when you buy in bulk.

Also, if you have room for inventory, buy seasonal items at the end of the season (for example, the day after Christmas) and hold them until the season comes around again to sell at a good markup.

Great Electronic Flea-Market Web Sites

1. AuctionHelper (www.auctionhelper.com)
2. Auction Wizard (www.auctionwizard.com)
3. InkFrog (www.inkfrog.com)
4. Sellathon (www.sellathon.com)
5. The Seller Sourcebook (www.sellersourcebook.com)
6. PowerSnipe (www.powersnipe.com)

For the Serious Online Seller

Building a solid customer base is much easier when you underpromise and overdeliver. Don't exaggerate the quality of the items you're offering. Tell the whole truth. In fact, it's better to err on the side of caution, pointing out even minor flaws. This assures people you're honest and prevents buyer disappointment. Always overestimate shipping times slightly so you aren't inundated with impatient e-mails from buyers. If you expect an item to arrive in seven to ten days, tell customers it might take two weeks. When it arrives in seven days, they'll be thrilled. Setting customer expectations just a notch lower than what you know you can provide will help you avoid disagreements, dissatisfaction, and negative feedback.

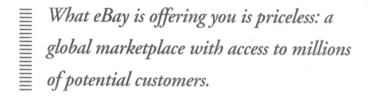

What eBay is offering you is priceless: a global marketplace with access to millions of potential customers.

Remember: Profit, Not Income

As with any business, you're in the online resale business to make a profit, not just to generate income. Run the numbers through your business plan to make sure you'll be making enough money to warrant your time. When you're calculating your prices, remember that at least 50 percent of auctions won't get a single bid. Yes, the competition is that fierce. So you may have to relist items several times before they sell—and each time you'll incur another listing fee. Determine the average number of times it takes an item like yours to sell by using resources like eBay's Marketplace Research. Then build those additional listing fees into your minimum price.

Some people resist selling through eBay because they don't want to pay the fees. But what eBay is offering you is priceless: a global market-place with access to millions of potential customers.

Drop-Ship

When you're making plenty of money and have built up a great fol-lowing of loyal customers, you'll be ready to go to the next level: drop-shipping. At this point, you basically act as a referral service for wholesalers or distributors. You choose products you want to represent, create the listing, automatically forward all orders to the drop shipper,

---

The Top Ten Tips for Selling Products Online

1. **Write a great headline.** You have to grab the buyer's attention.
2. **Post quality product images.** Eighty-three percent of eBay shoppers skip listings without images. Always put a product image right by the headline. You may need to post multiple photos from various angles.
3. **Accept PayPal.** PayPal is the currency of choice on eBay and craigslist.
4. **Write an interesting advertisement.** Make it a reflection of your personality, using wit and humor when appropriate.
5. **Price to sell.** The competition online is stiff. Hunt around to see what others are charging for similar products and cut your price 5 to 10 percent, but only if you can do so while still making a profit. Remember: You aren't interested in running a charity. You're in business. For bidding purposes, determine what you hope the final selling price will be and start the bid at 60 percent off. (Some experts recommend starting all auc-tions at $1 to attract a bidding war. If you do this, be sure to

and forget it. That's called passive income. Your eBay business puts money in your bank account while you're sleeping without any further involvement on your part. The profit per item is lower, but since you're selling a higher volume, your profits increase. (Remember, you're not after higher income; you're after profits.)

Think Long Term

Don't think in terms of maximizing your profit on one-time customers. Instead, seek to build long-term clients who return again and again. That

---

set a reserve price so you don't lose money.) If you're willing to accept a price that's around or below where it's selling elsewhere on eBay, list that price as the "Buy It Now" price.

6. **Offer a great deal and tell buyers why.** Say you're simplifying your life, and everything must go. Or your college grad is moving back home, and that's the end of your craft room.

7. **Tell the whole truth.** Inform buyers up front about any defects, so they can tell you're an honest person.

8. **Free shipping.** This is a great selling point, but be sure you're still making a profit.

9. **Be reasonable about shipping.** If you aren't offering free shipping, don't try to make a profit by overcharging for shipping. Be fair with your customers, or they may strike back and cost you future business.

10. **Have a star rating above 99 percent** If you follow the first nine tips, this shouldn't be a problem. Make sure you deliver what you say you will, when you say you will, and how you say you'll do it.

means providing great customer service by doing things like providing as much detail as possible about your products. Sell only items in great condition and be honest about flaws. Long-term thinkers also offer unconditional money-back guarantees and keep in touch with those who have ordered from them in the past, letting them know about related products and services.

> *Don't think in terms of maximizing your profit on one-time customers. Instead, seek to build long-term clients who return again and again.*

In every shipment, be sure to include a colorful flyer (black ink on bright-colored paper is cheap and effective) with a miniarticle related to the product, along with information about other items the customer may want to purchase. Even a shipping service will insert these for you, although they may charge a small fee for doing so. But since your best hope for future business is an existing customer, it's worth reinvesting in the business. That's what thinking long term is all about. As you become more sophisticated as an Internet/eBay auctioneer, you should definitely investigate auction-management software and other online resources that can automate your eBay business.

The great thing about eBay is that you can start small and reinvest your profits in the business for gradual but steady growth. Lots of people are making extra money, and some are making millions. There's plenty of opportunity, so why not join the world's largest flea market?

Questions ||||||||||||||||||||||||||||||||||||||||||||||||||||||||||||||||||||||||||||||||||||||||||||||||||||||||||||

1. Are you interested in holding a yard sale to generate some start-up cash for a home-based business? If so, set a date and begin searching your house for items to sell.

2. Do you need or want an eBay account? If so, when will you create an account? Set a date.

3. Have you invested time creating an "About Me" page and exploring eBay's online learning tools? If not, schedule that on your calendar.

4. Have you set up a PayPal account? If not, schedule that on your calendar. Everyone who sells (or buys) online should have a PayPal account!

5. Once you've learned the ropes on eBay selling used items, what product area might you want to specialize in?

Assignments ||||||||||||||||||||||||||||||||||||||||||||||||||||||||||||||||||||||||||||||||||||||||||||||||

1. List some family and friends who might allow you to raid their attics, garages, or storage units in search of products to sell. Put a date next to each name, indicating when you'll contact them.

2. Visit the suggested Web sites to learn more about making money on eBay. In the space provided, write a deadline next to each Web site, indicating when you'll explore its information.

Direct Sales and Network Marketing

In 1990, when I wrote *Homemade Business,* my first book on the subject of making money from home, I wasn't a fan of direct sales or network-marketing companies. I had seen people try and fail at direct sales after selling to their immediate circle of family and friends, having nowhere else to turn for potential customers. I had an even less favorable view of network marketing after some very negative experiences with deceptive representatives. The Internet has revolutionized the industry, however, and it provides both greater selling opportunities and more careful scrutiny of dishonest business practices. So now I'm a huge fan, as long as you begin with wisdom and proceed with tact. This might not be the right fit for you, but I hope you'll read on and consider it as one option for your home-based business plans.

Network marketing is only one type of direct sales. Network marketing "exists in at least 125 countries; it's approaching $100 billion in sales globally, driven by 35 million distributors worldwide."[1]

According to the Direct Selling Association,

Direct Selling is the sale of a consumer product or service, person-to-person, away from a fixed retail location. These products and services are marketed to customers by independent salespeople. Depending on the company, the salespeople may be called distributors, representatives, consultants or various other titles.[2]

In direct-selling companies, the person who does the work earns the money. You are rewarded for your hard work in direct proportion to your accomplishments, without regard to gender, race, education, or any other consideration. The cosmetic company Mary Kay has more than four hundred women who earn a six-figure income each year, and many of them don't even have a college degree. (If you'd like to learn more about the direct-sales companies I personally recommend, visit www.makingmoneywithdonna.com/direct-sales for a list.)

Sales is a field in which women have consistently excelled. Why? Because success in sales is a result of hard work and building relation-

---

To Learn More

Check out these online resources about network marketing:

- MLM Insider (www.mlminsider.com)
- *Network Marketing Magazine* (http://thenetworkmarketing-magazine.com/)
- *Network Marketing Business Journal* (www.mmmonthly.com)
- *Business Opportunities Journal* (www.boj.com)
- nmlifestyles.com (www.nmlifestyles.com)
- Dave Calvert's MLMSuccess (www.mlmsuccess.com)
- Doug Firebaugh's PassionFire International (www.passion-fire.com)

ships—two things at which women are particularly good. I have friends who've earned a steady income with a direct-sales business for twenty, thirty, and even forty years.

Direct sales also allows you to set your own hours and career pace. If you have children at home, your work can be done primarily in the evening when your spouse or friends are available to watch the children. If delivering products is part of your job, no one will mind if you bring the children along.

The Advantages of Direct Sales

Direct-sales companies offer all the advantages of being part of a larger organization, as well as the advantages of being your own boss. You work for yourself, but never by yourself. It really is the best of both worlds. You get to belong to something larger than yourself. You have a network of friends and peers. You have mentors who will teach you the ropes, help you set goals, and hold you accountable for achieving them. They will reward you and praise you to the highest heavens if you succeed . . . but they can't fire you if you fall short. That's a pretty good deal.

You Save Time, Money, and Work

Another huge advantage of joining forces with an existing business is that you don't have to start from scratch. The company has already researched and developed the products. They've already created all the promotional material you'll need and, in most cases, will provide you with your own Web site. It would take you many months and thousands of dollars to create this type of material for your own company. As an example, the network-marketing company I partner with invested $32 million in the replicated Web site that was available to me, at no charge, the day I became a distributor. I had previously spent hundreds of hours creating my own vastly inferior Web site. If I had to start all over again in a home business, I would definitely start with an established direct-sales company until I learned the ropes of entrepreneurship.

Direct-Sales Companies Often Offer Professional Development

The number-one advantage of joining a direct-selling company is the on-the-job sales-training and professional-development opportunities they provide. You simply cannot put a price tag on the value of that. Even if you ultimately want to start a business of your own, I would urge you to seriously consider signing up with a direct-selling company just to develop sales skills and to learn from marketing resources like seminars, teleseminars, conference calls, and so on. If you're going to succeed as a businessperson, you must learn to handle rejection gracefully and develop a thick skin. No one taught you that, did they? Well, a good direct-sales company will hold your hand and walk you through. You'll learn how to listen to "no, no, no, no, no, no" until you finally get to that great big "yes!" These skills are priceless.

Direct-selling companies have some of the most amazing conferences available anywhere, featuring top sales trainers and motivational speakers—people who charge $50,000 to $100,000 per speech! For a very reasonable fee, you'll get to learn from them. That right there might be worth the price of admission.

Choosing the Company That's Right for You

If you decide to get into the direct-sales world, you'll need to know some basics. Two major avenues of direct sales exist: person to person and party plan, which involves having a group of people gather at someone's home. Your personality determines which is right for you. Some people are too intimidated to speak in front of a group and would rather relate to people individually. Others find the party plan less stressful emotionally, because if one person isn't interested in your products, others in the group will help soften the blow.

> *If you're going to succeed as a businessperson, you must learn to handle rejection gracefully and develop a thick skin.*

The key to success is choosing a company and product line you believe in and feel good about representing. You should also consider how the products are delivered. In some instances, you have to deliver the products personally; other companies ship directly to the customer. One method isn't necessarily better than another; there are advantages and disadvantages to each. Company delivery is more convenient for you, whereas personal delivery offers more sales opportunities. Again, it depends on your preference.

Direct Sales Versus Network Marketing

Sometimes these two terms are used interchangeably, but there is an important distinction. All network-marketing companies are considered direct sales, but not all direct-sales companies use the network-marketing model. The term *direct sales* broadly means that products or services are sold directly by the salesperson to the consumer. But let me define the terms more precisely, and you'll see the distinction.

With a direct-sales company, you typically earn more money on each sale you make to your customers directly. The person who recruited you may earn a small commission. If you recruit others, you'll earn a small commission on their sales as well. But most of the profit goes to the person who makes the sale. The emphasis is on earning money in the

The Top Ten Questions to Ask Before Joining a Network-Marketing Company

1. *Where is the company's emphasis—on their great products or on how easy it will be to make money by calling people you went to grade school with?* Beware a company that pressures you to hurry up and recruit people before you've really experienced the products for yourself.

2. *Are the products unique and reasonably priced?* Overpricing is the kiss of death in today's economy, especially if the product doesn't address a compelling felt need. (People will pay a bit more for real solutions to felt problems. See question 3.)

3. *Do the products deliver measurable results, such as weight loss, visibly improved appearance, or increased energy?* There are some things people will pay extra for—specifically, health, wellness, and beauty.

4. *Does the company offer a range of consumable products?* One wonder product is rarely enough for long-term business success. Nonconsumable products make long-term customers and genuine residual income impossible. There are only so many home-decor or scrapbook supplies you can sell to your family and friends.

5. *Does the company offer free online training in the use and sale of the products?* Do they provide free online marketing tools, or are they still in the Stone Age, trying to sell you CDs and DVDs to hand out to your friends? Make sure the company is on the cutting edge of Internet marketing technology. The last thing you want is a company that still thinks the fax machine is a great way to do business.

6. *How much up-front investment is required?* It shouldn't cost

more than $500, including an initial product supply. Run as fast
as you can from a company that wants thousands of dollars
up front. I encountered one such company that suggested I
take out my credit card to buy into three nebulous "business
centers" for $5,000. Products were additional. No thanks.

7. *Are you required to sell an excessive amount of product each
   month to maintain your position and continue earning commissions?* A reasonable amount ($100 range) for personal use
   is fine. After all, you'd better use the product yourself, or why
   would anyone buy it from you? But you don't want to end up
   with a garage full of unsold products.

8. *Does the company make extravagant claims about the products or the potential income?* Companies that claim miracle
   cures or overnight riches are on the fast track to a review by
   the Federal Trade Commission. That's not something you
   want to be associated with. (If it sounds too good to be true,
   contact your state attorney general and the Better Business
   Bureau to see if complaints have been filed. A Google search
   might prove fruitful as well.)

9. *Do you believe in the products?* Do they address a felt need
   you've experienced? Did the products solve a problem or provide a real answer? Your most powerful marketing tool will be
   your own personal story of how the products have made a
   difference in your life.

10. *Could you talk about the subject behind the product (e.g.,
    beauty, health, fitness, etc.) all day, every day, even if no one
    paid you?* Do you have a genuine lifelong passion for the
    industry you'll be involved with, or will you be prone to burn
    out or boredom in a few months?

short term; therefore, immediate commission checks are usually higher with direct sales versus network marketing. Direct-sales companies, such as Creative Memories, Discovery Toys, and Tupperware, usually (although not always) market higher-ticket, one-time-sale, durable items like home accessories, toys, and scrapbooks. In those cases, repeat sales are usually fairly minimal.

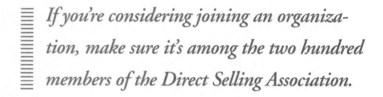

If you're considering joining an organization, make sure it's among the two hundred members of the Direct Selling Association.

Network-marketing companies, such as Amway, Herbalife, and Isagenix, typically offer retail commissions that are much lower, since more of the available commissions are directed toward bonuses paid to various up-line management people in the sponsor tree. You, in turn, earn commissions on a down-line of distributors.

Network-marketing companies usually offer consumable products designed for ongoing customer use. These reorders create what is called residual income. *Residual income* is money you earn from your initial sales and reorders, as well as the sales and reorders made by those you recruit, and the ones they recruit, and so on. This process can potentially continue to generate earnings for you long after you stop actively selling the products, assuming people like the products enough to continue using them month after month.

There are obvious advantages and disadvantages to each approach. Typically, it costs more money to get started with a direct-sales company, but you also earn more money more quickly. You can start most network-marketing businesses for less than $75, but it takes longer to build the business. Network marketing theoretically offers unlimited opportunity for exponential growth, but many people still have a negative view of the business so you meet with more resistance. Only you can decide which is right for you. You might want to do as I've done, and start one of each!

There are thousands of direct-sales companies operating in the United States today, offering everything from toys and clothing to cleaning and health-care products. Some are more reputable than others. If you're considering joining an organization, make sure it's among the two hundred

---

Is It Legitimate?

Many people believe that all network-marketing companies are pyramid schemes. That isn't the case. Nevertheless, there are some illegitimate companies out there, so you still need to be alert to possible problems. Here's the difference between a legitimate direct-sales or networking-marketing company and an illegal pyramid scheme: Legitimate companies emphasize selling products and recruiting others to sell them—they earn their money from selling product; pyramids emphasize recruiting others for their front money—they make their money from the fees new recruits pay them. It's against the law to run a business whose sole purpose is to recruit others who pay a fee who in turn recruit others who pay a fee, and so on and on. Of course, all multilevel marketing companies (MLMs) offer products, but if it's a fraudulent company, the products are only incidental.

Yes, you can successfully work at home through a direct-sales or network-marketing company. Just make sure you don't get roped into an illegal pyramid scheme instead.

members of the Direct Selling Association (www.dsa.org). If not, you might want to rethink it. This association hold its members to a high standard of integrity and accountability. For example, the member companies are required to buy back any unsold products from their distributors at 90 percent of retail value for up to a year. This ensures you won't be stuck with a garage full of unsold products—if it doesn't work, ship it back to the company. That's an important consideration. (See the sidebar, on page 105, "Is It Legitimate?")

Whichever direct-sales company you choose, remember that the 80-20 Rule applies here as it does everywhere else. The top 20 percent of salespeople earn 80 percent of the money. That's true in virtually every corporation. Your first question, then, is "Can I make it to the top 20 percent?" Maybe, maybe not.

So the second question is even more important: Is the business successful enough that the remaining 80 percent can earn a decent income? If it's a billion-dollar corporation, which many of these companies are, then ordinary 80-percent types can earn a nice stream of income. Not enough to buy a yacht or retire in Tahiti, but even if you earn just a few hundred extra dollars a month, isn't it worth it? That's a few hundred dollars you can invest. Just $250 per month, beginning at age forty, invested at 10 percent will yield $330,000 for your retirement at age sixty-five, and depending on the ups and downs of the stock market, you could even earn more.[3] Almost anyone can earn $250 per month with a reputable direct-sales or network-marketing company. Many people do much, much better.

Even if you work only two nights per week, you can surely earn some extra money for the family, and it will force you to develop your skills as a businessperson. I highly recommend it. (Since these opportunities are always evolving, visit www.donnapartow.com/social-networking ✱ for the latest recommendations.)

Questions ||||||||||||||||||||||||||||||||||||||||||||||||||||||||||||||||||||||||||||||||||||||||||||||||||||||||||

1. Do you have any sales experience? If so, describe.

2. Are you open to learning sales skills and developing the ability
    to handle the word *no* without falling apart? Where and how
    can you learn these abilities if you don't already have them?

3. Which sounds more appealing to you, direct sales or network
    marketing? Why?

4. Which industry appeals to you most?
    Home and family-care products
    Personal-care products
    Services
    Wellness products
    Leisure and educational products

Assignments ||||||||||||||||||||||||||||||||||||||||||||||||||||||||||||||||||||||||||||||||||||||||||

1. Visit the Direct Selling Association Web site, www.dsa.org. Note any companies you would like to explore in greater detail.

2. Visit the suggested Web sites to learn more about making money through direct sales and network marketing.
3. Write a deadline next to each Web site, indicating when you'll explore its information.

Information Products

If I had a dollar for everyone who told me, "I want to write a book," I'd take a cruise around the world. If I had a dollar for every man, woman, and child who dreams of writing a book, I'd own a fleet of cruise ships. My conviction is that everyone has a book buried deep inside.

Back when I started in book publishing—when we had to walk to school in the snow, uphill both ways—you either had to fight your way through a gauntlet in hope of landing a publisher or you self-published at great personal expense, and for the most part no one took you seriously. Option number one was often more like playing the lottery: Some won the big book contract and ended up smiling for television cameras, while everyone else lost. Option number two was more like putting your money in an incubator and praying it would miraculously multiply. Well, that's a slight exaggeration, but you get the idea!

Bottom line: Before the Internet revolution, if you wanted to share your message with the world, you needed to get permission. You needed a magazine or a book-publishing company to agree to let you use their presses to communicate with readers. Those days are over. Today, anyone can become a published author, and it doesn't have to cost you a penny. In fact, it can earn you money. Maybe even lots of it.

If you have a message you want to share with the world, create information products (also called digitally delivered products) and sell them online yourself. Every day, millions of people worldwide go online looking for information. You could be one of the many people cashing in on selling it. According to Yanik Silver, multimillionaire information marketer, "92 percent of what everyone searches for on the Internet is information."[1]

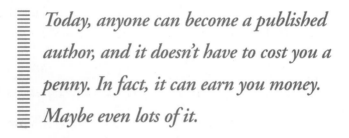

Today, anyone can become a published author, and it doesn't have to cost you a penny. In fact, it can earn you money. Maybe even lots of it.

The Internet provides you with the ideal way to trade your insights, opinions, and know-how for cold, hard cash. Do you know

- the secrets to a successful marriage?
- how to homeschool your children?
- how to save money on groceries?
- five ways to make holidays special?
- the best recipes this side of the Mississippi?
- a great way to lose weight and get in shape?

If you know anything at all that someone else might want to know, you can make money selling information on the Internet.

Think about your education, career, hobbies, and interests. Virtually anything you know can be turned into extra cash. And don't worry if you think you're not an expert. As long as you know more about the topic and spend more time researching than the average person, someone will pay for your information. Even if you don't believe you know anything, you can go interview someone who does. Or you can hunt down answers other people are providing in the form of information products and sell them via affiliate marketing (see chapter 9).

If you're going to turn your home into a lean, mean cash-generating machine (well, okay, forget the mean part), if you're going to succeed as a one-person home-based operation, you must remind yourself daily: Business success isn't about how much money you make; it's about how much money you keep. The distance between those two fixed points in your bank account is called *profit margin*. Some companies generate thousands of dollars in sales but fail to show a profit because their expenses are too high. Your goal is to keep expenses minimal.

> *Business success isn't about how much money you make; it's about how much money you keep. The distance between those two fixed points in your bank account is called* profit margin.

That's where information products come in. With information products, marketed over the Internet and delivered digitally, your overhead is negligible (maybe 3 percent in fees for services like Web hosting, autoresponders, and credit-card processing). Almost every penny you make is profit. The other great thing about information products is that they require minimum up-front investment, involve little financial risk, and once created, provide entirely passive income. I encourage everyone reading this book to develop at least one information product as part of an overall moneymaking strategy.

Developing Information Products

Based on your answers in chapter 5, list ten topics you have enough knowledge about or interest in to create a book or a blog. For each of the ten, list ten subtopics. For example, if you love photography, subtopics might include wedding photography, photojournalism, and how to take great photos. Don't rush through this step; give it careful consideration. Take out pen and paper, or better yet, sit down at your computer. Once you have one hundred subtopics (also known as keywords) listed, you'll be ready for the next step.

The Top Ten Great Things About Information Products

1. Great profit margins
2. Best-selling product category on the Internet
3. Create it once, and your work is done, yet you keep earning indefinitely.
4. There's nothing to ship.
5. There's no inventory to track.
6. No personal selling is required.
7. There's minimal interaction with customers.
8. It's passive income—money will appear in your checking account while you're sleeping.
9. You can recruit others to market your information products by establishing your own affiliate-marketing program.
10. The sales of your information products can position you as an expert, enabling you to earn even more money through seminars, teleseminars, and e-courses.

Looking at your topics and subtopics, comb through your lists to pick the one area where you feel you have the most material to work with. Consider the topic for which you were able to quickly come up with ten subtopics. It should also be one with solid keyword search results. (In chapter 12 I'll explain all about keyword search results and creating blogs.) For now just remember you can develop an infinite number of information products and market them through an infinite number of blogs. It's important to create a new blog for each information product you want to sell.

Don't confuse potential buyers by flooding them with information about a dozen unrelated topics or products. They came to you for a specific reason. That's all they want to know about. Some popular topics for information marketing include the following:

- Self-improvement and self-help
- Health and fitness
- Weight loss
- Alternative medicine
- Music lessons
- Art lessons
- Parenting and child development
- Business-to-business training
- Sales and marketing training
- Investing
- Personal finance
- Real estate
- Dating advice
- Relationship advice
- Pet care and training
- Anything an identifiable group of people want to know about!

Free Information

At the heart of information-product marketing is, ironically, free information. For example, you might offer a free "Tip Sheet for Expectant Mothers." By giving away your free information, you lay the foundation for financial success by building your mailing list of prospective customers. In traditional business marketing, you have to go looking for customers. With Internet marketing, prospective customers come to you. Think about it. The moment someone contacts you, asking for the free "Tip Sheet for Expectant Mothers," you know she is probably an expectant mother. If you provide her with helpful insight, she will quite likely reward your efforts by purchasing from you. If you ask her when her baby is due, you can market age-specific products to this mother for the next eighteen years.

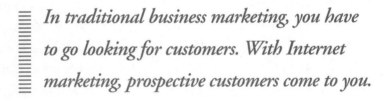

In traditional business marketing, you have to go looking for customers. With Internet marketing, prospective customers come to you.

It's a fair exchange: your valuable information in return for the e-mail address of a potential customer. Once the person has entered his or her e-mail on your blog page, your computer can automatically send the information to their in-box. (The best way to do this is via a system called an *autoresponder*, which we will cover in chapter 12). Don't ask people for too much information. Do you need their last name to send them a free e-mail? No, all you need is an e-mail address. You can also ask for their first name so you can personalize your e-mails. Do you need their home mailing address? Whatever for? If the person purchases a product from you, you'll need that information, and at that point, he or she will gladly give it to you. But at this early stage of the game, remember that people value their time and are rightfully cautious giving out too much personal information over the Internet. Be reasonable and respectful; prospective customers will be more likely to exchange preliminary information if you are.

Once your prospective customer has provided you with an e-mail address, you can send him or her the requested free information. In addition, you can also tell this new contact about the next item in your information-product series; namely, a special report.

Special Reports

Your first income-generating information product should be a special report. A special report on a particular topic need be only ten to twenty pages, and you can price it at $7. Now, I don't personally know the psychology behind $7 and why it's such a strategic number, but the slogan among Internet marketers is this: If someone will give you $7, she'll give you thousands. Is it true? I have my doubts, and frankly, the slogan sounds cynical and along the lines of P. T. Barnum's famous maxim "There's a sucker born every minute." As Christians, we're not trying to milk a gullible customer, but instead we want to provide a worthwhile, meaningful experience for the customer so that he or she gets valuable information, and you, in turn, get a positive response and the potential for return business. Nevertheless, since $7 is the going rate for starter products, just go along with the flow.

Remember: It costs you nothing but time and creativity. Your goal is volume. Imagine if one thousand people needed and subsequently purchased your $7 special report. When you consider that there are millions of people surfing the Internet, that's not an unreasonable goal.

I recently heard of a homeschooling mom who wrote a special report on "How to Raise Leaders." She posted it on the Internet and earned $10,000 in a matter of days. I don't find it hard to believe that fifteen hundred parents in the world want practical ideas for raising leaders. I'd find it hard to believe if there weren't.

Coming back to the example of expectant mothers, your $7 special report might be titled "101 Ways New Moms Can Save Money." Fill the report with creative ideas, plus links to great money-saving Web sites, free product samples, and special offers you arrange with reliable companies. Be sure to include valuable coupons that make it well worth the expectant mother's $7 investment. If you do, you'll have won a new friend and a loyal customer.

Can you think of a compelling topic—one you can become an expert on—that thousands of people want to know about? Of course you can! Think. Research. Pray. Try an idea. Then try another idea. And then another. Information marketers are making millions; my guess is you'd be content with thousands. You can do it!

Again, the amazing thing about the Internet is that it is absolutely free to publish your special reports. You risk nothing but your time. What if you set a goal to create one twenty-page special report every week? You'd have to create only four pages of material per day, five days per week.

Notice I said create; I didn't say write. You don't have to be a great writer to create special reports. You don't even have to come up with original material. Scour the Internet and other sources and compile information that's already been written by others (just as if you were writing a research paper). Then distill it down into the simplest possible terms by implementing the following ideas:

- Translate it into plain English—something a fourth grader can read is ideal.
- Break up the information into bite-size chunks.
- Put the information into checklists and charts.
- Create implementation strategies.
- Share examples from your own life.

- Be careful not to plagiarize, and make sure to give credit where credit is due by documenting your sources! Just because information is on the Internet doesn't make it public domain. And, because you are *selling* the information, you need to be especially careful not to steal intellectual property. Run, don't walk, to your public library and check out a copyright handbook to see what steps you must take to legally market copyrighted information.
- Include resource boxes listing books, magazines, e-zines, Web sites, and blogs to go to for further information.

People will gladly pay $7 just to have all the links they need to pre-screen Web sites in one place. Even if your material isn't entirely original, you're providing a valuable service by compiling all this information for the reader's convenience.

E-Books

An e-book is a downloadable electronic book. While local bookstores are going out of business, online e-book sales are booming. People love the affordability and convenience of clicking a few buttons to have the book delivered directly to their e-mail's in-box. They can then either read it on their computer screen, print it out, or both. Some popular secular topics for e-books include the following:

- How-to tips on any subject whatsoever
- Self-help
- Goal setting
- Time management
- Internet marketing
- Selling on eBay
- Finances—making, managing, and investing money
- Moneymaking ideas
- Money-saving ideas
- Health/beauty/fitness/diet

- Aging well, antiaging, longevity tips
- Education, homeschooling, adult learning, skills training
- Travel
- Lifestyle

Ten Steps to Creating Your Own E-Book

For step-by-step guidance to creating and selling an e-book on the Internet, visit www.makingmoneywithdonna.com/e-books. ✳ Following are ten basic steps to take:

1. Choose a superspecific topic that solves a problem or answers a vital question. Check keywords first to make sure there's a viable market.

2. Research your topic.

3. Create an outline using ten subtopics for ten chapters.

4. Write a five- to ten-page chapter on each topic, for a total of fifty to one hundred pages. (Lots of bullets, boxes, graphics, charts, and lists are fine.)

5. Quote experts and statistics. List relevant Web sites, books, and other sources.

6. Recruit a few extra sets of eyes to read through your e-book. It's easy to miss your own mistakes.

7. Design a professional-looking front cover and interior page layout on the computer. There's lots of free software on the Internet that will enable you to do this. Simply Google "create e-book covers" or "free e-book covers" and check out what's currently available.

8. Save the e-book as a PDF file, and lock the file so readers cannot cut and paste it into another computer file. You can find free "add-ons" that enable you to do this with your

- Wedding planning
- Parenting, new parents
- Pregnancy
- Women's health

word-processing software. Download the free Adobe Acrobat Reader software from the Internet. To enable your word processor to interact with Adobe, simply Google "save as PDF file" and download the add-on program. Then when you click "Save as" in your word processor, you'll see the option of "Save as PDF."

For Microsoft Word, go to http://office.microsoft.com /en-us/word/HA100649921033.aspx. You can even password protect your document to discourage people from sharing your e-book with others. To password protect your PDF document (after you have saved it as a PDF and you have it open in Adobe) go to Advanced > Security > Encrypt With Password. A prompt will appear asking if you are sure you want to change the security settings. Click on Yes. Select "Encrypt all document contents," check "Require password to open document," and enter the password in the "document open password" field. If you want control on the permissions to print and edit the document, check "Restrict editing and printing."

9. Write at least two bonus special reports to offer alongside your e-book. People love bonuses!

10. Create an information-product blog specifically for your e-book. Load your e-book PDF into a shopping cart that delivers it directly to customers via e-mail upon purchase.

Faith-based topics are fine too. These can include Bible studies, prayer guides, Sunday school curriculum, and the like. It may seem unspiritual to charge for these, but remember that pastors get paid to distribute information in the form of a sermon, and Christian book writers make money on their books.

Subscriber Newsletters and Membership Sites

People will pay you to do all the latest research for them, particularly when it comes to money-saving ideas, increased efficiency, better sales, or a greater return on financial investments. Even if you charge just $9.95 a year, with one thousand subscribers, you can quickly earn an extra $10,000 a year. Not bad.

Or you can create a private Web site where you share ongoing information and coaching to people for a one-time or monthly fee. For example, my Exclusive Access Club offers women an opportunity to study with me personally for three months. I charge anywhere from $27 to $97, depending upon the program, and have had hundreds of women enroll.

Audio Information Products

If you aren't comfortable writing, make up a list of interview questions, call into free Internet radio Web sites like Talkshoe or BlogTalkRadio with a friend, and have her ask you the questions. Answer as thoroughly as you can, and you've instantly created a marketable product. How? Sell the interview as a downloadable audio. It's free and easy to create audio products with Talkshoe or BlogTalkRadio. Record a series of these interviews, and you can market it as an e-course, training others to do what you've done. It's a very popular and lucrative Internet option, especially if you can train people how to make money. I've used both Talkshoe and BlogTalkRadio to record audios that I sell as part of my e-classes.

After you've recorded your program to create an audio product, you can take the next step. Either transcribe the audio yourself or hire some-one to do it for you. The Web site iDictate (www.idictate.com) offers transcription services for a penny a word. Now you can sell not just the audio but the transcript as well. With a bit of editing, you might even be able to turn it into a marketable e-book.

Your Information-Product Blog Needs Only Four Pages

The following Web pages are all you need to advertise your infor-mation product on your blog:

1. **Sales page.** Include a compelling description of your product with emphasis on problem(s) it will help the reader solve and/or questions it will answer.

2. **Download page.** Once the buyer submits his or her payment information via your online shopping cart, your site should automatically redirect the buyer to a page containing link(s) to download the product(s) just purchased. This information can also be sent via e-mail.

3. **Thank-you page.** After the buyer has downloaded the item(s), the system should redirect him or her to a thank-you page. Here you can thank the buyer for the purchase and also sug-gest another related item he or she may want to buy. This is typically a more expensive item but one that also offers a great value. *Remember:* Just because something is expen-sive doesn't mean that it's overpriced. The more expensive the item, the more it should benefit the purchaser.

4. **"About Us" page.** Include information about you, your com-pany, and your policies on this page.

Video Products

Another great option for creating information products is video. I took out my ten-year-old video camcorder, blew off the dust, and set up a makeshift studio in my living room. I created a series of two- to seven-minute companion videos to go along with my book *Becoming the*

Moonlighting on the Internet

While researching this book, I stumbled upon Yanik Silver's excellent resource for those who want to start moonlighting on the Internet while keeping a day job. In it he lists the following nine criteria for evaluating a possible Internet business:[2]

1. **A Huge demand.** Pick something almost everyone is interested in, such as saving or earning money or improving health or happiness.

2. **No need to bother your friends.** The surest way to end up in the NFL (No Friends Left) is choosing a business that relies on selling to your family and friends.

3. **No inventory.** If you're working this business only at night, you don't want something that involves shipping and storing products. It's just too overwhelming.

4. **No employees.** Moonlighting or working full-time, I concur that life is too short to spend it managing employees!

5. **Residual income.** Develop a business plan that allows you to create an information product just once, put it up on the Internet, and let it sell itself while you're sleeping.

6. **Low cost and low risk.**

7. **Low maintenance.**

8. **No need to be supertechnical.**

9. **Real business (not some scam).**

Woman God Wants Me to Be. I posted these on YouTube and Facebook for free, just to generate interest in the product. Then I began selling them as part of a $97 Internet class. We also compiled the collection onto two DVDs, which we sell for $37 via my blog and at my speaking engagements.

Recently I purchased the Flip video camera (it cost $199 plus tax), which features built-in software that posts directly to many social-networking sites like Facebook and YouTube. The technology to create video products will continue to improve and become more accessible and affordable for home-based business owners.

I just introduced a new Internet course, based on my book *Becoming the Woman I Want to Be,* featuring companion videos recorded at home using my Flip. Nearly two hundred women signed up within the first week for a fee of $27 each. I'm so glad I spent that $199.

Questions ||||||||||||||||||||||||||||||||||||||||||||||||||||||||||||||||||||||||||||||||||||||||||||||||||||||||||||||||||||||

1. Have you ever said, "I want to write a book"? If so, what topic or topics interest you?

2. What topic (or topics) do you have a passionate interest in that might lend itself to an information product?

3. What free information product could you develop to kick-start your information-product marketing efforts?

Assignments |||||||||||||||||||||||||||||||||||||||||||||||||||||||||||||||||||||||||||||||||||||||||||||||||||

1. List potential topics for special reports.

2. List potential topics for an e-book.

3. List potential topics for bonus offers.

4. List potential topics for audio and/or video products.

9

||||||||||||||||||||||||||||||||||||||

Affiliate Marketing

Not long ago, I received a notice from PayPal that $900 had been deposited into my account. That's a nice e-mail to wake up to! What made it even better is that it wasn't for one of my own products. No product expense, no overhead. There was nothing to ship, no work to be done. There was nothing to do but spend the money, which, fortunately, I'm very good at.

Where did the money come from? Affiliate marketing. I had simply included a link on my Web site to a real-estate training program that I recommended. People had clicked the link and purchased the training program, and then the business owner paid me the promised commission. It's called affiliate marketing, and you can do it too.

It's easy to get involved with Internet marketing, even without developing your own product or service, by specializing in affiliate marketing. Affiliate marketers don't sell their own products or services. Instead, they serve as informal representatives for a wide variety of other Web-based marketers. Major corporations, from Apple to Zappos, have spent millions developing affiliate-marketing programs. Why? Because they are profitable for everyone involved. The customers win because they find the information and product they need. The companies win because you send customers their way. You win because you get paid for influencing people (through accurate, reliable information sharing) to buy a particular reputable product or service.

Basically, you earn referral fees. This has got to be one of the most passive ways ever devised to make money. You never even interact with the customers. You could be sound asleep when someone in China clicks a button and stumbles onto your Web site or blog, and then clicks another button that takes him or her to a Web site offering products you recommend, and then clicks another button to buy the product. Three clicks and you're getting paid. It doesn't get much easier than that.

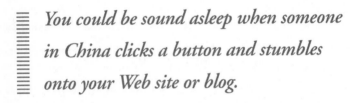

You could be sound asleep when someone in China clicks a button and stumbles onto your Web site or blog.

The most obvious example is Amazon.com. You can create an informative Web site or blog about a topic of interest to you—say, for example, cooking. Then you provide a list of recommended cookbooks and a direct link to Amazon. Amazon stocks the books, ships the books, bills the customer, and pays you. That's what passive income is all about: earning money while you sleep. Of course, affiliate marketers have to provide links to lots of Web sites if they hope to make significant income. Or you can do as I've done: Use affiliate marketing as just one of your strategies for generating multiple streams of income.

There are three ways to earn money through affiliate marketing: pay per click, pay per lead, and pay per sale.

1. Pay per click. Interestingly enough, you can even get paid if the person doesn't buy anything. Some companies will pay you for every person you send their way who clicks around on their site. Not much per click, but it might just add up.

2. Pay per lead. You'll earn a little more from companies who pay per lead. Your referral becomes a qualified lead the moment the individual provides the merchant with information about him- or herself via an online form.

3. Pay per sale. Obviously, the highest commission rates are earned when someone you've referred actually purchases the product you suggest.

Although it would seem that you'd make the most money from pay per sale, that isn't always the case. People do a lot more clicking than buying. All those little clicks and completed forms can add up even faster than actual sales. Why not try all three approaches to earning money through affiliate marketing?

Getting Started

To begin, turn back to chapter 5 once again. Take another look at your education, career experience, talents, hobbies, and other things you enjoy thinking, talking, or writing about. What types of products would someone like you want or need? Imagine you're the customer now. What would you like to purchase related to any or all of the potential businesses you identified? What do you need to know to make sure your purchase is a solid bargain? Make a list. Now you just need to track down companies that are offering those types of products via affiliate programs.

One of your lists might look something like this:

- Tennis
- Tennis balls
- Tennis rackets
- Tennis shoes
- Tennis apparel
- Tennis coach
- Tennis tournaments

- Tennis elbow
- How to win tournaments (e-book idea)
- Improve your serve (e-book idea)
- Avoid common tennis injuries (e-book idea)

Commission Junction

Your first stop should be Commission Junction (www.cj.com), currently the one of the largest and most reputable affiliate-marketing clearing-houses. This is where you'll find traditional retail-store products like tennis equipment, clothing, shoes, and more. It takes only a few minutes

---

The Top Ten Affiliate-Marketing Tips

1. Choose a reliable affiliate clearinghouse and let the company do the initial work of separating the wheat from the chaff.

2. Stay focused on items related to your core business concept. Don't be distracted by the vast array of goods and services offered.

3. Start slow. Look for a few traditional products with a good profit margin and one or two information products that pay a 50 percent commission. Resist the temptation to sign up for a boatload of affiliate programs.

4. When you're ready to expand, select a broad range of products within your niche.

5. Be sure to pick items in all price ranges, from a few dollars to a few thousand.

6. Don't inadvertently promote fraudulent businesses or useless information products. You'll kill your credibility. Check everything out. You can contact the Better Business Bureau

to create a free account. One excellent feature of Commission Junction is that it tells you, up front, the average earnings per one hundred clicks so you can choose accordingly. Of course, don't choose a product simply because someone else is making money with it. Choose a product you can get excited about recommending to others.

Once you've chosen the products you want to recommend, you'll need to cut and paste banner ads onto your Web site or blog. Then when people click, fill out a form, or buy a product, you'll earn some extra money from home.

Of course, if no one comes to your Web site or blog, there won't be

---

or simply do a Google search to see if anything troubling turns up.

7. Buy and try products yourself so you can sincerely endorse them.

8. Remember, people buy based on emotion. Your sincere enthusiasm is your best marketing tool.

9. Research the company and the people behind it. Even if their products are great, it does you no good if they cheat their affiliates out of commissions. Again, in the age of social networking, this is easily done. You might even ask on Twitter, "Has anyone worked with such-and-such affiliate program?" People will be quick to tell you if they haven't gotten their affiliate commissions!

10. Don't be afraid to rewrite the suggested promotional material to suit your personal style. The information products, in particular, sometimes include incredibly tacky hit-you-over-the-head sales tactics.

much clicking going on. Your mission is to drive as much traffic as you can to your site to maximize the clicking. You'll find help with that process throughout the remainder of this book.

ClickBank

Speaking of clicking, a great place to find electronic products and services to recommend (for example, how-to e-books or Internet-based training programs) is ClickBank (www.clickbank.com), a clearinghouse for online affiliate products. You can set up a free account and then browse through countless thousands of e-product listings. Be sure you

---

Ten Tips for Success on the Publishing Side of Affiliate Marketing

If you've developed your own information product, you can dramatically expand your sphere of influence while multiplying your income by recruiting affiliates to promote your product. Here's how to go about it:

1. **Choose a powerful topic.** Address a pressing felt need experienced by a large group of people.
2. **Research the market.** Will people pay for the type of information you're selling?
3. **Pick an irresistible title.** You can't go wrong with "How to . . .," followed by a specific benefit.
4. **Write a compelling sales page.** You must convince potential affiliate marketers that people won't be able to resist buying your information product.
5. **Be easy to find.** Place your product in the right category and use accurate keywords.

believe in the product and study the company behind it before you begin spreading the word.

The top products are those that teach people how to make money. There is a certain irony that people are making millions telling other people how to make millions by telling other people how to make millions. (See more in the following section, "Warnings Before You Start Affiliate Marketing.") Nevertheless, if you want to succeed, be sure to choose a topic people are willing to invest money in. Think training rather than just informing or entertaining.

ClickBank collects payment over its secure server, delivers the

6. **Be patient.** Don't expect an army of affiliates to join you overnight. It may take six months to a year before your information product gets noticed.

7. **Market with diligence.** Do at least one thing every day to spread the word to potential affiliates about your information product.

8. **Price it right.** Your information product should be priced reasonably enough so that end users will buy it, but high enough so that the potential profit will motivate affiliates to market aggressively to their e-lists.

9. **Offer a 50-50 percent split to your affiliates.** It's passive income for you, so don't be greedy!

10. **Recognize that the competition is fierce.** There are literally hundreds of thousands of information products on the Internet. Your product had better be unique and deliver real solutions. Spend more time developing the product than you do trying to recruit other people to sell it. Ultimately, the product must sell itself by delivering on your promise.

electronic product to the buyer, monitors all earnings, and pays both the product creator and all affiliates via direct deposit each week (or a twice-monthly check, if you prefer). Now that's what I'd call a lazy person's dream business!

Warnings Before You Start Affiliate Marketing

A few warnings are in order. You should know that there are some deceptive companies in the affiliate-marketing business who will accept your referrals and never pay you a dime. This is what I call the Internet version of envelope stuffing. You remember those envelope stuffing ads that said you could make big money stuffing envelopes? When you sent money for the information on how to make money, they gave you instructions on how you could place an ad promoting envelope stuffing. In other words, no one ever stuffed envelopes. (Machines can do that at a rate of a zillion envelopes per second—hello!) It was just a scam. Garbage like that abounds in the world of affiliate marketing.

The other problem is hype. Spend an hour reading some of the information products on ClickBank, and you'll see what I mean. There are countless e-books for sale that promise the moon but really contain very little substance. Particularly in the area of making money on the Internet, there's far more heat than light. So stay alert. Thoroughly research every product you recommend to make sure it delivers real value and not just fluff.

Setting Up Affiliates to Market Your Products

Thus far, we've looked at earning money by referring customers to products or services you recommend. But there is yet another way to earn money with affiliate marketing. That's by recruiting affiliates to market your products and services. You can set up a simple program whereby you'll pay your affiliates a commission fee for sales they drive to your Web site. Your main goal should be to find affiliates who will reach people you wouldn't otherwise be in contact with. (In other words, you don't want to pay people to compete with you.)

You can start with just a few affiliates, and if you find it's profitable and not difficult to manage, you can expand from there. Remember that affiliates are like having your own sales force, and they represent you and your company to the world. That's good news, but it also means you need to choose your partners carefully. You don't want someone out there giving you a bad name.

To set up your own affiliate program, you can go to ClickBank.com and upload the information about your product.

Questions ||||||||||||||||||||||||||||||||||||||||||||||||||||||||||||||||||||||||||||||||||||||||||||||||||||||||||||

1. Which of your chapter 5 items looks most promising as the basis for an affiliate-marketing business?

2. What products did you discover on Commission Junction that you might want to refer customers to?

3. What information products did you discover on ClickBank that look worthy of offering as an affiliate?

4. Do you see potential to develop your own products or services to offer via an affiliate program? If yes, list potential products to sell.

Assignments |||||||||||||||||||||||||||||||||||||||||||||||||||||||||||||||||||||||||||||||||||||||||||||||||||

1. Set up a Commission Junction account. Do it now or set a date to get this done.

2. Set up a ClickBank account. Do it now or set a deadline!

3. Also explore Affiliate Scout (www.affiliatescout.com) and AffiliatePrograms.com (www.affiliateprograms.com). Write your notes here:

Part III

||||||||||||||||||||||||||||||||||||||||||||||||||||||||||||||||

Business Basics

Misty Taggart has been working from home for almost thirty years. For most of that time, she worked as a freelance screenwriter in Hollywood. Misty, who was mentored by William Hanna of the famed Hanna-Barbera Studios, always loved her work. What she didn't enjoy was the terrible Southern California traffic. Working from her Hollywood home, she could avoid that, except for studio meetings.

When she retired from the Hollywood scene, she was looking for a way to create a new business that would bring the same creative satisfaction in a completely new location. She began exploring home-business ideas that would build on her decades of experience while offering her greater independence and more time at home.

Misty remembers, "I wanted to carve out a niche for myself that would put me in demand so customers would come to me." In 2008 she founded Trailer to the Stars!—a production company through which Misty (and the team of freelance, also home-based experts she partners with) writes, produces, and distributes promotional videos for new book releases. Her clients are authors, publishers, and public relations firms. "Our objective is to create short, intriguing videos that are the number one marketing tool for our clients. We post them on dozens of social media outlets, ranging from YouTube and Tangle to Facebook and Twitter."

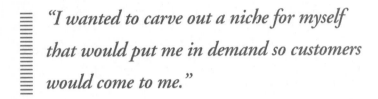

"I wanted to carve out a niche for myself that would put me in demand so customers would come to me."

Although Misty is the creative, artistic type, she still conducts herself like a professional. She admits, "Even though I absolutely love the fact that I can go with the flow when my creativity is on a roll, or walk away when I hit the wall, I still have to be disciplined in certain ways." For example, every morning she gets up and gets dressed, including fixing her hair and putting on makeup. "I never go into my office in my pajamas. I think that's a huge mistake. I need to feel like I'm really going to work. I want to feel like I'm ready to meet my clients even if it's over the phone or via the Internet."

She also says, "The professionalism of the work must speak for itself; it must be of the same caliber or even better than anything produced in a traditional office. You have to take yourself and your work seriously."

Of course, working from home is now mainstream, and there's no longer the stigma that was once attached to it; in fact, working from home is chic. Misty agrees. "My clients don't even think about where I work, except maybe to wish they worked at home too. The Internet has changed everything."

Misty also takes full advantage of the latest technology. "I have clients throughout the United States and Canada. Also in England, Australia, and New Zealand. With Skype I can communicate with them face-to-face without leaving home." She has a state-of-the-art Web site—www.trailertothestars.com—and makes use of social networking, blogging, article marketing, and other strategies we'll be exploring throughout the pages of this book.

> *"My clients don't even think about where I work, except maybe to wish they worked at home too."*

Misty has clients lined up for the next six months, so she is clearly doing something right. Her advice for those who are interested in making money from home? "You're going to have really, really good days and really, really depressing days. With no one there for you, it's tempting to quit. But you have to persevere and find a way to be self-motivated. Self-motivation is key. You have to treat yourself the way a real boss would treat you, or you'll never make it. Truth is, I'm tougher on me than any boss ever was, because I know what I'm capable of, and I have in no way achieved all of my goals just yet."

Legal and Financial Issues

Kimber King (from page 5) began to pay more in taxes than she had made in total the previous seven years—what a problem to have! Many potential home-based entrepreneurs are scared off by legal and financial hurdles and red tape—but they are essential skills to develop. I won't sugarcoat things by telling you that legalities and paperwork aren't a hassle. However, the amount of red tape will be determined by the size, complexity, and nature of your business. My advice: Keep it simple. If you don't take out a loan or hire employees, the legal issues you must tackle remain minimal. There's no need to assume that kind of risk in today's marketplace. Thanks to Internet technology, you can start very small ($500 to $1,000) and gradually build over time.

Like legal issues, business finances may be unknown territory for the new home-based businessperson. However, once the terms are understood and a few points are clarified, finances become far less daunting. Hopefully this brief overview will familiarize you with some commonly used financial terms and practices.

Choo∫ing a Legal ∫tructure

The first legal decision you will have to make is what type of structure your business will assume. Realistically speaking, your two choices are sole proprietorship or a limited liability corporation.

Sole Proprietorship

This model offers substantial benefits for the home-based businessperson, and in the vast majority of instances, this structure should be chosen. You won't incur any legal fees because there are no forms to file. You simply register with the city or county clerk, as discussed in the following paragraphs, a task you can certainly do without legal assistance. You need to obtain a d/b/a ("doing business as") or trade-name certificate from your local or state commissioner's office. Typically, that will not cost a lot. The cost varies by state. The fee can be as low as $1; the average is about $25.

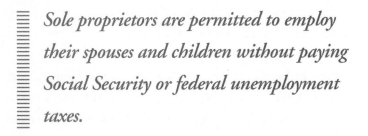

Sole proprietors are permitted to employ their spouses and children without paying Social Security or federal unemployment taxes.

Sole proprietors are permitted to employ their spouses and children without paying Social Security or federal unemployment taxes. That isn't the case for a corporation. Chances are, your family will end up on the payroll at some point, so this is an important benefit. Another advantage is that your sole proprietorship can simply cease and desist without filing any paperwork whatsoever.

Under a sole proprietorship, all profits and losses are attributed to you personally. So if your business will involve taking major financial risks (which I hope it won't), you should seriously consider adopting a corporate structure. Otherwise, you'll just need to file Schedule C, "Profit or Loss From Business," when you file your 1040 federal tax form at the end of the year. If you earn more than $400, you'll also have to file Schedule SE, "Self-Employment Tax."

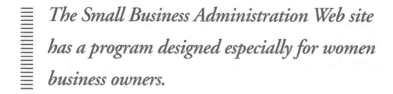

The Small Business Administration Web site has a program designed especially for women business owners.

You can find out more about starting a sole proprietorship on the Internet; search for "starting sole proprietorship" or peruse the Small Business Administration Web site (www.sba.gov). The latter has a program designed especially for women business owners.

Limited Liability Company (LLC)

If you have $200 to invest, it's worthwhile to form a limited liability company. It provides the benefits of a sole proprietorship (you're still taxed as an individual) and a corporation (limiting your personal liability in the event of a lawsuit). If someone sues your company, they can take only company assets. They can't take your house or anything else that belongs to you personally. In today's litigious society, that's something to think about. You might start out as a sole proprietor, but as your company grows, you could graduate to an LLC. (For more information on legal structure, check out the Small Business Administration Web site.)

Setting Up Legal Shop as a Business Owner

There are several things you need to do when starting your business or moving it to the next level. Take these seriously and don't cut corners. Establishing a serious business will help motivate you to put professional effort into it.

Choosing and Registering a Trade Name

If you elect to operate as a sole proprietor, you are permitted by law to operate under your personal name. However, if presenting a professional image is important to you, then it's advisable to choose an official trade name for your business. When starting an LLC, you also have to choose a trade name. Keep in mind that banks won't allow you to open a business account until you have a trade-name registration certificate in hand.

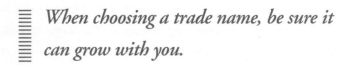

When choosing a trade name, be sure it can grow with you.

When choosing a trade name, be sure it can grow with you. The name Apples-R-Us may seem cute now, but what if you start selling oranges? On the other hand, if you are a toy maker and won't be expanding into other areas, a name that clearly identifies what you do is best. Contact your county clerk's office or other government entity to learn the procedures for obtaining a d/b/a or trade name.

Registering a Trademark

Trade names and trademarks are different—you want to register both. After getting your trade name secured, you'll have to do a trademark search to find out if anyone else has your trade name. Go to the Trademark Electronic Search System (TESS) to search for trademarks registered in the United States. Or you can do a trademark search in person at any Patent and Trademark Depository Library (PTDL). Search the PTDL Web site to find one in your state.

Register your trade name as a trademark. You may never need it, but better safe than sorry.

Opening a Post-Office Box

When you register your trade name, you'll be asked to provide a business address. Keep in mind that this address will become public knowledge, and within several days, you can expect to receive a truckload of mail from people who want to sell you products and services. It may be advisable to open a post-office box in your company's name to prevent the dissemination of your home address.

Opening a Bank Account

One of the first things you must do is open a checking account. Having a separate business checking account is an excellent way to ensure that good records are kept, because deposits represent your income, and checks or other withdrawals represent your expenses. If you will be conducting business under any name other than your own, be sure to bring your trade-name (d/b/a) certificate and several forms of identification.

Getting a Sales Authorization Certificate

Most state governments (and many municipalities) levy a sales tax on merchandise. If you sell or resell a product, you'll need a sales authorization certificate. This assigns you a resale tax number so you can buy material wholesale and not have to pay sales tax on it until it is resold, either incorporated into your final product or as is.

You must collect sales tax on everything you sell directly to consumers in your home state, and then remit the money to the appropriate government office. The percentage varies from state to state, so contact your state department of taxation, sales tax bureau, for more details.

Obtaining Necessary Licenses and Permits

Depending on the nature of your business, your state or local government may require you to obtain certain licenses or permits before you begin operation. For example, a hairstylist requires a license, and daycare facilities may need special permits. If you're unsure of the requirements for your particular line of business, contact the Small Business Administration. Few Internet-based businesses will require any type of license or permit.

Observing Zoning Regulations

Most states, counties, and municipalities have zoning restrictions on the types of businesses that may be conducted in certain areas. For example, you probably won't be permitted to board horses or open a beauty salon in your suburban housing complex. If your business will involve nothing more than your sitting at your home computer, and no clients will ever come to your house, then zoning isn't an issue. But if you plan to allow customers to come to your house for any reason, you need to do your zoning homework. If customers will be parking their cars in front of your neighbors' homes, and those neighbors object, you could have a real problem on your hands. (Another reason why I advise meeting with customers elsewhere.) If in doubt, contact your local Small Business Administration office.

Purchasing Insurance

Be sure to contact your insurance agent to discuss necessary changes to your policy. This is particularly important if you plan to invest in office equipment or will need to maintain inventory in your home. Some of the issues you should discuss include the following:

1. Fire, theft, and casualty damage to equipment and inventory
2. Liability coverage for customers, vendors, or others who may visit your home business
3. Product liability coverage if you make or sell a product
4. Professional liability if you will be offering a service
5. Additional car insurance if you plan to use your family vehicle for business purposes

Your insurance agent will almost certainly require a copy of your business plan. Also, be sure to ask if you're entitled to a discount on your homeowner's policy, since working at home much of the time reduces the chance of fire and burglary.

Be sure to ask if you're entitled to a discount on your homeowner's policy, since working at home much of the time reduces the chance of fire and burglary.

Taxes

One of the great advantages of having your own home business is the amazing tax savings. Historically, the American government has understood that entrepreneurship is the backbone of our economy. So tax laws were written in such a way to reward those who are willing to take risks and to encourage entrepreneurial activity. When it comes to taxes, you are expected to pay your fair share. Paying more is foolish and unnecessary. As a self-employed businessperson contributing to our economy, you are entitled to certain deductions; don't be afraid to make use of them. You aren't taking advantage of the system; you are the reason the system was created. Never forget that.

You aren't in business to generate income. You're in business to generate a profit. Big difference! Your business income equals the money that comes in to your business. Get it: Income = what comes in. But if all that money goes right back out in the form of taxes, it doesn't do you or your family much good, does it? Your goal is to keep as much of that money as you can in your bank account rather than transferring it to government coffers. The money that sticks around is called profit. Your goal is to maximize your profit by minimizing taxes and other expenses.

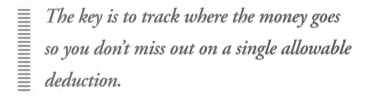

The key is to track where the money goes so you don't miss out on a single allowable deduction.

The key is to track where the money goes so you don't miss out on a single allowable deduction. I have used the computer software Quicken for years to track my businesses; another popular option is Microsoft Money. Both are inexpensive and easy to use. It may take a few hours to set it all up and link the software directly to your business checking account (which you should open as soon as you have your d/b/a certificate in hand). Once you've set up your categories, tracking deductible expenses is easy and virtually automatic.

When to Pay Taxes

By the time you file your tax return, you should have paid 80 percent of your total income tax and Social Security tax due for the year. This is accomplished by filing Form 1040-ES, "Estimated Tax for Individuals," and paying the estimated tax based on how much you have earned over the preceding three months. The deadlines for quarterly filings are April

15, June 15, September 15, and January 15 of the following year. Your state government may also require quarterly filings.

The Tax Implications of Using Subcontractors

I would urge you not to hire employees for your home business. Instead, rely on independent contractors; that is, people who will work for you on their own time and declare their earnings directly to the government. You don't deduct any taxes from their earnings, and you're required only to give a Form 1099 to any independent contractor who earns more than $600 in a given year. The government is very strict about this! Don't think you can treat someone like an employee and then call him or her a subcontractor. Learn the difference between the two by completing IRS Form SS-8, "Determination of Worker Status for Purposes of Federal Employment Taxes and Income Tax Withholding," and viewing Form 8919, "Uncollected Social Security and Medicare Tax on Wages." (See www.irs.gov/pub/irs-pdf/fss8.pdf.)

Is It a Home Business or a Hobby?

How does the IRS decide whether you have a legitimate home business or you're just trying to write off expenses related to a hobby? Simply put, you must show that you intend to make a profit. As a rule of thumb, the IRS says your business should show a profit three of five consecutive years. However, even if you don't make a profit three out of five years, you can still demonstrate that your business is legitimate if you carry on your activities in a businesslike fashion—keeping financial records and following normal business procedures, demonstrate that you have (or are developing) expertise in your field, and keep careful records of time invested.

This distinction is extremely important. If your activity is a hobby, you can deduct expenses related to the activity as an itemized deduction subject to the 2-percent-of-adjusted-gross-income limitation, but you cannot deduct more than the income from your hobby. However, if your activity is a business, you can deduct all of your expenses. If your expenses exceed your business income, you can deduct the excess from other income. And that will make a big difference in your total tax liability.

A Word of Warning About Taxes

Please be aware that tax matters are extremely complex. This section was designed to provide some tips but is by no means intended as a complete guide to taxes. You should consult a tax expert who can help you with your specific questions. IRS Publication 587, titled *Business Use of Your Home*, outlines the income-tax regulations specific to a home-based business. Visit the site www.irs.gov/publications/p587/index.html for helpful information. The Web page for the Small Business and Self-Employed Tax Center—www.irs.gov/businesses/small/index.html—is also handy. It provides a wealth (pardon the pun) of information on the tax laws pertaining to home businesses. You can even download the necessary forms. You can also return to the Small Business Administration Web site at www.sba.gov. It offers a comprehensive listing of their small-business programs and publications, along with reports, statistics, and studies related to various fields of endeavor.

Tax Deductionſ for Home-Buſineſſ Ownerſ

Business-use-of-home deduction. If you use part of your home exclusively or regularly for business and it serves as your principal place of business, you're entitled to deduct costs as a business expense. *Exclusively* means that portion of your home that is used for business and nothing else. You cannot deduct your bedroom or kitchen if you use part of it for business and part of it for family. The deduction is allowable only if you have an entire room set aside for business.

The one exception is inventory storage. For example, if you use half of the basement to store products, you can deduct it. You may also deduct for other facilities located on your property, such as a greenhouse, an artist's studio, or a garage, if they're used solely for business purposes.

Regularly means that even though you don't devote your full time to conducting your business at home, you do so on a regular basis. Your home is your principal place of business if you spend more than 50 percent of the time devoted to a particular job at home. (In other words, your home can qualify even if your business is a side job.)

> *If you use part of your home exclusively or regularly for business and it serves as your principal place of business, you're entitled to deduct costs as a business expense.*

The deduction allowed is based on the percentage of your house used. The most acceptable way to determine this is to calculate the square footage of your office as a percentage of the entire square footage of your house. Or you can approximate using the following method: Let's assume you have a three-bedroom house with a dining room, kitchen, and living room, and all six rooms are approximately the same size. If one of the rooms serves as your office, you can deduct one-sixth of your mortgage or rent. (For more details, visit the IRS Web site www.irs.gov/taxtopics/tc509.html and read Topic 509, "Business Use of Home.")

Indirect home-office expenses. You can also deduct the same percentage of your real-estate tax, electricity, home-owners insurance, and so on, as a business expense. Even putting on a new roof, painting the exterior, and other such renovations and repairs are all considered indirect expenses related to your business and are partially deductible based on the percentage.

Direct home-office expenses. Directly related expenses, such as painting or carpeting your office, are fully deductible.

Travel. Whenever you take a trip for the sole purpose of conducting or promoting your business, all expenses—airfare, car rental, lodging, meals—are fully deductible.

Entertainment and business gifts. You can also deduct a portion of the cost of lunches, dinners, theater tickets, and the like, incurred while cultivating clients or prospective customers. A five-minute discussion with your best friend about how things are going does not constitute a business lunch. The event must be directly related to the active conduct of your business.

Education and training. If you attend seminars, classes, or conventions to further your business skills, you can deduct fees, tuition, and books, as well as transportation and incidental expenses.

Local transportation. When you run general business errands—to the store or a client's site, for example—you're entitled to deduct mileage, parking, and tolls. Or you can deduct a percentage of gas, oil, tires, insurance, repairs, or even the cost of a new car. (To determine the correct percentage, keep track of how many miles are used exclusively for business and how many miles were traveled overall throughout the year.) Please note that you cannot have it both ways. You may use either the per-mile deduction or the percentage method. If you use H&R Block TaxCut, TurboTax, or other tax-planning software, it will calculate both options and let you choose whichever gives you the larger deduction.

Research events. Any time you take a trip to acquire information necessary for your business, whether it's to the local library or to check out the competition, the expenses you incur are deductible (mileage, parking, library materials).

Donations. If you donate one of your products to charity, such as a handcrafted vase, the actual worth (not the sale price) of the item is deductible.

Regular expenses. Any expenses you incur in the regular course of business are fully deductible, including all technological gadgets for your computer (and your monthly Internet service charge) and your cell phone (as well as the portion of the bill attributable to your business phone). But don't forget the little things, which can add up: tape, envelopes, postage, paper clips, pens, stationery. And don't overlook the biggies either, such as advertising expenses, business cards, and office equipment and furniture. Whenever possible, pay for business expenses by check or debit card and obtain receipts. Taking an extra minute to write an explanation on the back of the receipt will be a tremendous help when tax season rolls around.

Questions

1. What are the advantages of a sole proprietorship for your business?

2. What are the advantages of an LLC for your business?

3. Which legal structure will you adopt?

Assignments ||||||||||||||||||||||||||||||||||||||||||||||||||||||||||||||||||||||||||||||||||||||||||||||||||||

1. List ten possible names for your business. Now begin to narrow it down until you find the right one. Remember to make sure the name isn't already a registered trademark of someone else. (*Warning:* This might take a lot longer than you think. Be sure to get opinions from family and friends as well.)

    _____   _____

    _____   _____

    _____   _____

    _____   _____

    _____   _____

2. Check on zoning laws, if warranted.
3. Open a post-office box, if desired.
4. Register your trade name with the city, county, or state clerk.
5. Apply for applicable licenses or permits.
6. Talk to your insurance agent about your business needs.
7. Open a business bank account.
8. Complete your projected budget.

Mastering
Self-Management

When I talk with women about starting a home-based business, one of the most frequent objections I hear is, "I couldn't possibly find the time." Yet many women spend thirty or forty hours a week away from home and still manage to keep the household running smoothly. This objection points to an underlying fear that they wouldn't get anything done without a boss hovering over them or a production schedule driving them to meet deadlines.

There's little doubt that your business will fail unless you learn to use your time wisely. Working at home provides many distractions and temptations that could pull you away from your business. How effectively you use your time will largely determine how successful your business becomes.

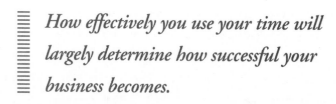

How effectively you use your time will largely determine how successful your business becomes.

Conduct a Time Inventory

Begin by conducting a time inventory. This will help you determine how much time you have for a home business and may point out some areas where you can save time. (I've done this exercise countless times since 1982, when I read Michael LeBoeuf's book *Working Smart: How to Accomplish More in Half the Time.*)

Re-create the Time Inventory Chart at the end of this chapter or download it at www.makingmoneywithdonna.com/time-inventory. Then, for one week, carry the chart with you and jot down how you spend the better part of each half hour (e.g., watching TV, talking on the telephone, washing dishes, etc.). But don't suddenly spend two hours in prayer just to make yourself look good; be honest and try to follow your normal routine as much as possible.

If you're anything like me, this will serve as shock therapy! It may be disconcerting to realize how much of your time is spent on trivial pursuits. Still, the idea is to discern where your time is wasted and strive to recapture it. For me, time flies when I'm on the phone. Like many people, I have a tendency to continue talking long after the usefulness of my words has ceased. If this is an area you struggle with, you may want to keep a close watch on your phone calls. It might be helpful to set your kitchen timer each time you pick up the phone, and whenever possible, limit your conversation to a predetermined amount of time.

Carry an Organizer

One of the best ways to use waiting time, and to manage your time in general, is by carrying a personal notebook or electronic organizer with you at all times. I'm addicted to my BlackBerry, but I also carry a paper notebook just because I'm old-fashioned. Remember, your home business will only be as organized as you are.

The Top Ten Ways to Conquer Time Wasters

As a self-employed business executive, you can no longer afford to allow time wasters to control your life. The following tips may help you redeem your time:

1. **Have a daily quiet time.** Ironically, one of the best ways to save time is to spend time. Each morning, set aside a quiet time of Scripture reading, reflection, and prayer. This investment will pay rich dividends throughout the day by giving you wisdom to deal with clients and make good decisions.

2. **Learn to say no.** Many women find this difficult. Somehow we have the idea that declining any request for our time and assistance is unspiritual. Nonsense! Jesus didn't respond to every request while He walked the earth. Yet He was able to say to His Father, "I have brought you glory on earth by completing the work you gave me to do" (John 17:4). As Charles Hummel points out, Jesus was able to do so because "He discerned the Father's will day by day in a life of prayer. By this means He warded off the urgent and accomplished the important."[1]

   We need to be clear about our calling and purpose. Our top priority, of course, is our relationship with God. And for wives and mothers, the second priority must be providing and caring for both the physical and spiritual needs of our families. Be sure to keep first things first. Then if you have time and energy to bake five dozen cookies for the church picnic, terrific. But don't feel you have to comply with every request. That's a recipe for disaster.

3. **Avoid perfectionism.** When good enough is good enough, it's good enough. Is it absolutely necessary to spend seven

hours raking the backyard to remove every last leaf when the yard looked okay after an hour? The way I see it, life is too short to waste fussing over minor details.

4. **Remember Parkinson's Law.** Work expands to fill the time available for its completion. It even expands to fill time that's not available. Especially when it comes to housework, there's always more that could be done. I realize this is a matter of personal preference, but strive for balance in this area.

5. **Stop procrastinating.** Charles Hummel says it best: "Unanswered letters, unvisited friends, unwritten articles, and unread books haunt quiet moments when we stop to evaluate what we have accomplished."[2] My most exhausting days are the ones in which I've accomplished the least, because frustration and regret sap all my strength.

   If a job needs to be done, it's much better to tackle it and get it over with. Then you'll have the satisfaction of crossing it off your to-do list. If your business is going to succeed, you'll have to exercise the spirit of self-discipline (2 Timothy 1:7). That means pacing yourself to do a little each day rather than letting things get out of control before you take action.

6. **Stop stewing.** Most of us would agree that too much of our precious energy is dissipated in bouts of worry, anger, and bitterness. Don't allow business difficulties to make you anxious. Worry is a waste of time. Pray about the obstacles you're facing, but don't worry about them (see Philippians 4:6-7).

   Starting a business requires faith and trust in God's provision, so look at it as an opportunity to grow in these areas. If you find yourself getting discouraged, one of the wisest time

investments you can make is memorizing Scripture to coun-
teract negative thought patterns.

7. **Stop shuffling papers.** Paper has a way of invading even the
most well-ordered homes. Junk mail, magazines, newspapers,
newsletters, and the like are insidious time wasters. Make it a
rule to handle each piece of paper that crosses your desk
only once, if at all possible. Act on it, clip it, file it, or throw it
away, but don't spend all your time shuffling around the same
old papers. Better yet, cancel all those subscriptions and opt
out of direct-mail campaigns by visiting the National Do Not
Call Registry (www.donotcall.gov).

8. **Tame the telephone and television.** Decide how much time
you're willing to spend each day on the two Ts, and ruthlessly
stick to it. Just this week a study revealed that the average
American watches five hours of television per day. That's more
than enough time to run a successful home business! Just
think, all the time you used to devote to watching game
shows can now be channeled into your business endeavors.
And which will yield greater rewards?

9. **Schedule shopping trips for off-peak hours and seasons.** This
is particularly important if your business will involve shopping
for supplies often. Also, keep those trips to a minimum by
maintaining a list of things you need and buying in bulk.

10. **Make the most of your waiting time.** Rather than reading the
tabloid headlines when you're standing in line at the grocery
store, pull out your to-do list and bring it up to date or jot
down any brilliant ideas that come to mind. Do the same
while you're waiting at the dentist's office or bus stop.

Is your house scattered with little slips of paper reminding you of things you're supposed to do or people you have to call? Or worse, is your head cluttered with thoughts like *What was I supposed to do today? What's the deadline for my project? What time does that meeting start?*

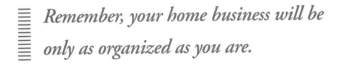

Remember, your home business will be only as organized as you are.

You can get rid of your jumbled thoughts and scattered notes by transferring everything into your organizer. In a home-based business, your personal and business lives are intricately intertwined. An electronic or paper organizer will help balance and organize all the competing demands in your life.

Goal Setting

Goal setting empowers you to make the most of each day by putting the power of focus on your side. When I say goals, I don't mean the resolutions you talk about on New Year's Eve and then forget by January 15. I'm talking about goals that stay with you throughout the year and impact the way you live each day. If you've never set any goals for yourself, now is the time to do so.

Sit down and begin to think and pray about what you want to accomplish in your life. These are your *lifetime goals* and may include things like "establish a successful home business employing five other women," "write a book," or "provide college tuition for the kids."

Once you have a good idea of what you want to accomplish in your lifetime, determine what you need to do this year to begin making those goals a reality. These constitute your *yearly goals* and should be more specific. If your lifetime goal is to write a book, your yearly goal may be to write the first five chapters. Or if your lifetime goal is to establish a successful business, this year's goal may be to finish reading this book and decide which business is right for you.

Finally, there are *daily goals*, which are the most specific of all. In other words, if your lifetime goal is to be a godly person, and your yearly goal is to read through the Bible, you can do so by reading four or five pages per day. Most of the women I know think they could never find time to read the Bible in one year. It seems overwhelming, but don't you think you could read five pages in one day?

If you want to write a book during your lifetime and plan to write five chapters this year, your daily goal may be to write one page per day. That doesn't sound so hard, does it? That's the advantage of breaking down your goals into manageable tasks: Things that looked impossible suddenly seem achievable.

It's important to write out your goals and review them frequently. Sunday is a particularly good day to reflect upon the prior week and evaluate how your time and energy were spent in relation to your goals. The Weekly Evaluation Worksheet at the end of this chapter will assist you through this process. A time of reflection will help keep your priorities in focus and ensure that you attend to the important, not just the urgent. (Should you desire to make use of the Weekly Evaluation Worksheet on a regular basis, it's available as a downloadable PDF at www.makingmoneywithdonna.com/weekly-evaluation-worksheet.)

The Fine Art of Delegation

From time to time a lot of women feel like slaves to their families, serving as cook, chauffeur, maid, and coach all rolled into one. Unfortunately, they feel that they alone must do everything involved with running their households and end up wearing themselves out. That is where delegation comes in.

If you have children in the home, in view of all you do for them each day, it isn't unreasonable to expect them to contribute to the smooth operation of their own household. Don't underestimate their ability to help out around the house. Even small children can and should be taught to clean up after themselves. Yet how many women spend hours each week picking up after Junior? That's not only bad management; it's bad parenting, because it produces irresponsible children. Older children can be given responsibilities such as meal preparation, dish washing, and gardening. That doesn't mean you turn them into a band of slaves and render their lives not worth living. But it does mean instructing children in the lost art of responsibility.

Mother's Helpers

Even with the assistance of your children, there may be additional household chores that should be delegated so you can devote more time to your business. Proverbs 31:15 says that the wife of noble character provides "portions for her servant girls." Most women zip right by this verse, thinking it's irrelevant to their lives. After all, who could possibly afford to hire servants? But I truly believe the concept of "servant girls" or mother's helpers is an almost universally overlooked resource for today's busy mothers. I propose hiring a junior or senior high school student (a girl is usually best unless you have all boys) to serve as your special assistant around the house. She can help out with babysitting, cooking, cleaning, and errands.

Where can you find such an assistant? First, look to your neighborhood. Perhaps there is a young girl living nearby who would be interested in earning some extra money. (If not, you're living in a very unusual neighborhood!) If you don't have any luck there, try your church youth group or local school.

Let me urge you to view this arrangement as more than just a moneymaking opportunity for your helper and a convenience for you. Young girls yearn for role models, and what an opportunity for you to model the Christian life! You may have a profound, even eternal, influence on her life as you speak wisdom and faithfully instruct her as the Lord leads (see Proverbs 31:26). As part of your witness, be sure to give her the "portion" she has earned and encourage her to be a wise steward of her income.

But wait, you may be thinking, *If I have to pay someone to keep an eye on the kids or clean the house, how am I going to make a profit?* If you worked outside your house, you'd have to pay someone to watch your children, wouldn't you? This arrangement will almost certainly cost you less, and you won't have to worry about whether or not your child is receiving good care. And, of course, you'll be immediately available if a problem arises.

> *In view of all you do for your children each day, it isn't unreasonable to expect them to contribute to the smooth operation of their own household.*

For the most part, you'll be working side by side as a team. Your helper may be doing the laundry while you work on an article you hope to publish. Or she may play quietly with the children in the backyard while you're on the phone scheduling appointments.

When my children were young, I found this arrangement extremely beneficial. One teenager came over regularly to help with housecleaning, and a twelve-year-old girl frequently played with my infant daughter while I worked on business projects. If either of my daughters needed me, or if I just wanted to take a hug break, we were always close to each other. And because I was always close at hand, these girls became not

only my employees but special friends as well. I recently attended both
of their weddings.

In order to make the principle of delegation work for you, bear in
mind two basic guidelines. First, be sure to hire good help. If your next-
door neighbor is always complaining about how lazy and difficult her
daughter is, the girl is probably the wrong candidate for the job. Second,
your assistant will be only as good as the training and tools you provide.
Let her know exactly what is expected, and take the time to teach her.
Don't just hand her a bucket of cleaning supplies and go on your merry

---

Five Bonus Time-Management Tips

1. **Set annual and lifetime goals.** What could be worse than coming to the end of your life and realizing you've pursued someone else's dreams? Set your own goals and then choose a
   home business that will enable you to achieve them. Remember: A goal is a dream with a deadline. Put it in writing. The
   more specific, the more likely you are to achieve it.

2. **Establish checkpoints.** Researchers surveyed people over the
   age of ninety and asked them how they would use their time
   differently if they could live all over again. The top three
   answers: "I would reflect more," "I would risk more," and "I
   would do more significant things." Each week set aside one
   hour to reflect on the activities of the prior week and to plan
   the coming week. That way you can ensure that you take cal-
   culated risks and do significant things.

3. **Carry a daily planner.** Today's market is flooded with organiz-
   ers—both electronic and paper. As I've said, I personally use
   both: my BlackBerry for my address book and other contact
   information, and my paper notebook for planning and life

way. That's a formula for misunderstanding and is almost guaranteed to generate ill will on both sides. Training will be time consuming at first. You'll probably be frustrated by the realization that you could get the job done more quickly (and better) yourself. But investing a little extra time now will save you a great deal more in the future.

As you seek to implement these time-saving strategies, realize that some of these tips will work for you; others may not. The important thing is realizing that you really do have enough time to establish and operate your own home-based business.

---

management. The most important consideration: Can you carry it with you at all times? Use your daily calendar to set daily priorities and keep first things first. Ask yourself, *What small thing must I do today to move closer to my larger goals?*

4. **Develop good habits.** Put the power of momentum on your side. Set up systems for doing routine tasks in a specific way, at a specific time, in a specific place. Create "activity centers" for correspondence, phone calls, accounting, and so on, complete with all the necessary supplies and equipment. Then you won't waste time looking for needed items or wondering what to do when and how.

5. **Apply the 80-20 Rule.** Nineteenth-century economist Vilfredo Pareto observed that a small percentage of any activity yields the majority of the results. You will find that 20 percent of your clients comprise 80 percent of your business; 20 percent of your products yield 80 percent of your profit, and so on. Focus your energy on the 20 percent that will do the most good and forget the other 80 percent. You'll actually work less and accomplish more.

Questions ||||||||||||||||||||||||||||||||||||||||||||||||||||||||||||||||||||||||||||||||||||||||||||||||||

Once you've completed a week-long time inventory (see the Time Inventory Chart on page 166 or download from www.makingmoneywith donna.com/time-inventory), answer the following questions:

1. How and when did I waste time?

2. What activities can be reduced, eliminated, or delegated?

3. Did I attend to the truly important, or merely urgent, things in my life?

4. Does my schedule reflect my priorities?

5. Am I using my time to achieve the goals I've set for myself?

6. Whom did I talk to on the phone? Were the calls important and necessary?

7. Did the phone conversations continue beyond necessity? Could they have been shorter and still effective?

Assignments ||||||||||||||||||||||||||||||||||||||||||||||||||||||||||||||||||||||||||||||||||||||||||||||||||||

1. Buy and set up your organizer.
2. Make a list of goals in the space below.

3. Hire a helper. Make a list of five teenagers you can contact about becoming your helper. If you don't know of any, contact your church youth leader or local homeschooling group. A homeschooled student could be available during the day all year rather than just during the summer months.

Time Inventory Chart

Week of _____

Time	Mon	Tues	Wed	Thurs	Fri	Sat	Sun	Activity
6:00 AM								1. Spiritual
6:30 AM								2. Read
7:00 AM								3. TV
7:30 AM								4. Phone
8:00 AM								5. Groom
8:30 AM								6. Cook
9:00 AM								7. Eat
9:30 AM								8. Dishes
10:00 AM								9. Sleep
10:30 AM								10. Clean
11:00 AM								11.
11:30 AM								12.
12:00 PM								13.
12:30 PM								14.
1:00 PM								15.
1:30 PM								16.
2:00 PM								17.
2:30 PM								18.
3:00 PM								19.
3:30 PM								20.
4:00 PM								21.
4:30 PM								22.
5:00 PM								23.
5:30 PM								24.
6:00 PM								25.
6:30 PM								26.
7:00 PM								27.
7:30 PM								28.
8:00 PM								29.
8:30 PM								30.
9:00 PM								
9:30 PM								
10:00 PM								
10:30 PM								

Weekly Evaluation Worksheet

1. What did I study in my quiet times this week?

2. Which of my business and personal goals did I pursue?

3. Which of my goals did I fail to pursue?

4. Did I attend to the important or merely urgent?

5. Am I using my unique gifts to develop my business?

6. Am I spending time in my office each day?

7. How's my business going?

8. What specific goals do I have for the coming week?

Part IV

Marketing Your Business

Rosey Dow is the mother of seven children and an Internet marketing expert. She began working from home back in 1982 as a full-time author, whose credits now include fourteen published books and the coveted Christy Award for Christian fiction. Her writing career first expanded to radio and television appearances, and then speaking at writers' conferences. Today she directs ChristianFictionMentors.com, a twelve-lesson interactive program that guides new writers through their first novel, and also the CEO of Experts in Focus, an online promotion company that trains authors how to get their work out to the world using Internet technology and social networking.

Her first foray onto the Internet was a traditional Web site, which she launched in 1998, but she admits, "No one ever came to it!" That changed in 2007 when she became a student of Internet marketing. She recalls, "I started out with article marketing. I realized that online articles are so much quicker and simpler to write. Unlike conventional articles, getting published online is a breeze. All you have to do is submit your work to free article directories. I found that I could easily write three articles a week, and then just add a resource box inviting people to come to my Web site. All of a sudden, my Web site started getting traffic."

> *"Unlike conventional articles, getting published online is a breeze. All you have to do is submit your work to free article directories. I found that I could easily write three articles a week."*

She was able to convert some of that traffic into sales of her traditional books, but she gradually realized that e-products were even more profitable for her. "With an electronic product, there's either no cost or very little cost involved. It's almost all profit. Best of all, once you set it up, it's passive income. I earn money while I'm homeschooling four of my children. Or even while I'm sleeping. Once I discovered that, I knew I'd found my niche with information products."

Her next step, after article marketing, was launching a blog in the summer of 2007. She says, "Things really kicked into high gear once I realized I could connect my blog with Facebook and Twitter. I started seeing more interaction with people coming to the blog, becoming my friend on social networks, and turning to me as a resource for advice on Internet marketing."

To keep up with the growing interest, especially from fellow authors who wanted to know how to harness the power of the Internet to market their books, Rosey became a dedicated student of Internet marketing. "I was determined to learn all I could, not just for myself, but so I could teach other authors," she says. She invested $10,000, attending both live conferences and online training programs to position herself as an expert on Internet marketing.

Through these and other strategies, Rosey began capturing names and e-mail addresses. This enabled her to keep in touch with customers and prospective customers through the use of autoresponders and e-zines. As of this writing, Rosey has an incredible 5,800 Twitter followers and 2,800 Facebook friends!

Her advice to others who want to explore Internet marketing? "It's vitally important for you to become a student. Tackle one thing at a time. Start with blogging and learn it well. Then when you've mastered it, move on to article marketing. You can easily become overwhelmed learning a little about a lot. So learn a lot about one aspect at a time." She also warns, "Don't wait until you've got it all figured out. Don't be afraid to make a mistake. You learn by doing. Jump in and give it a try. Put everything you learn into practice immediately. Don't be forever learning and never applying."

Rosey says she loves teaching others about Internet marketing because it forces her to stay on top of trends: "In this Internet world, if you stop learning, you're gonna get run over or left behind." Rosey teaches an outstanding online class (I know because I was her student!) called Information Profit Secrets. It's a five-week program (two hours per session) offering a crash course on teleseminars; article marketing; social networking; how to develop products, including special reports and e-books; Internet radio; and so much more. Rosey puts it this way: "I give students a step-by-step strategy for creating an information empire." (You can learn more from Rosey at Experts in Focus [www.roseydowtoday.com].)

Rosey says one secret to her success is that she treats her home business like a real job. "I get up every morning and report to work. My family knows I'm at work from 9:00 AM to 1:00 PM daily, and they've learned to respect that. Even if you work only two to four hours a day, you can make a lot of progress if you stay focused on the high-priority tasks that yield the greatest return."

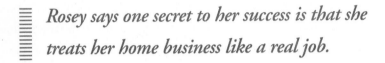

Rosey says one secret to her success is that she treats her home business like a real job.

Today Rosey is enjoying great returns from her multiple streams of income, including her novel writing, Christian-fiction mentoring program, conference speaking, online teaching, and sales of her downloadable training modules for passive income. Rosey also offers an annual information-marketing conference and serves as an online marketing consultant to fellow authors.

Everyone Needs a Blog

It's been said that a blog in the twenty-first century is what a horse was in the eighteenth century: a way to get anywhere you want to go to see and be seen. *Blog* is short for "Web log," and creating one is much easier than designing a traditional Web site. You can set up a blog, free of charge, in less than an hour. (For a comprehensive video tutorial, visit www.makingmoneywithdonna.com/blog-tutorial, and you'll be walked through all the steps outlined in this chapter.)

Even if your business won't be exclusively Internet-based, you still need an Internet presence. A blog is a virtually free way to build your credibility and boost your potential for business success. I recommend that everyone in a home-based business have a blog to make a statement about your product, make a difference, and make some money. Even if you don't want to publicize your life, your views on your product establish your expertise and will help you develop credibility.

In the blogosphere, the maxim "Content is king" rules the day. What is content? It's information of any kind: words, pictures, videos, and audios. You expand your blog by adding new content in the form of "posts," which shouldn't take more than an hour per day to create. You can even post to your blog from your cell phone, as I found out on a recent missions trip. Driving on dirt roads in rural Mozambique, I was able to keep everyone back home updated just by sending posts directly from my phone to my blog. It was amazing.

When you add a new post, it jumps to the top of the front page of your blog. All prior posts get pushed down, so your blog appears in reverse chronological order. The key to success is constantly creating fresh content by updating your blog at least three days per week, preferably more. (See the section "Get Found—Search-Engine Optimization" later in this chapter.)

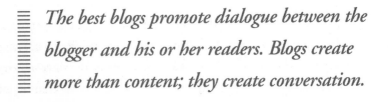

The best blogs promote dialogue between the blogger and his or her readers. Blogs create more than content; they create conversation.

In addition to your own posts, your blog can include links to other sites on the Internet. But what really drives the blogosphere is that, unlike traditional Web sites, visitors can become active participants in the discussion. The best blogs promote dialogue between the blogger and his or her readers. Blogs create more than content; they create conversation.

The best blogs incorporate multimedia. A blog is like a

- bookstore—offering books, e-books, and magazine articles to read
- TV or movie studio—offering videos to inform or entertain
- radio station—with access to online talk shows or downloadable MP3s
- photography studio—featuring photos related to your niche
- retail store—where you can sell products
- business—providing services to potential customers

- wholesale distributor—recruiting others to retail your product for a commission (see "Affiliate Marketing," chapter 9)
- news outlet—where people can find out all the latest news
- watercooler—where colleagues gather to discuss business trends
- town hall—where anyone can debate the issues of the day
- community center—giving like-minded people a place to chat

Now consider that a blog can do all of that for *free* (or virtually free), instantaneously, around the world. It's no wonder the blogosphere is taking off!

now for the Good news

Remember back in the introduction when I told you the bad news about Web sites, like oDesk, that link corporations with skilled workers in developing countries? Well, there's still good news. Here's what someone in a foreign country cannot do for $2 an hour: He (or she) can't be you. He can't have your exact passions, your life experiences, your interests, thoughts, and feelings. And that person can't express them in your unique, God-given way.

That's why I believe there's still plenty of opportunity for people like you and me to succeed in the global economy. A blog is a way for you to share what you care about with the world—the whole world.

To succeed as a blogger, all you need is a topic that interests you and at least a few thousand other folks. It helps if you're smart and/or funny. Preferably both. You can write your own content or simply become a resource person who gathers information from other sources. A simple way to do that is by downloading a special Web tool—"Get the Button"—from ShareThis (www.sharethis.com). Then as you surf the Net and find articles related to your niche, simply click and share. If you've got money to invest and feel confident your idea will fly, you can hire a writer at Elance (www.elance.com).

Pick Potential Blog Topics

Flip back to chapter 8, "Information Products," and review your list of topics and subtopics. Next, go to Wordtracker (www.wordtracker.com) and plug in each of the one hundred subtopics. If the average daily search for the topics is around one thousand per day, you have a viable subject for blogging. The higher the number of searches, the greater the interest in the subject.

Add up the total interest for each of the ten potential blog topics. Based on the results from Wordtracker, you can narrow down your ideas for a potential blog by eliminating the bottom half. Other good sources include Google's free keyword research tool at https://adwords.google .com, along with Good Keywords (www.goodkeywords.com).

Go to Google to see who is already offering what. If no one is advertising for that keyword (look on the right-hand side of the page under "Sponsored Links"), then the idea is probably a dud. If a good number of companies are already paying for that keyword in search engines, evaluate what they are offering to see if what you plan to offer is distinctive enough.

Another great way to gauge interest in your subject is Amazon.com. Go to the Web site, type in your keyword, and see how many books come up on the subject. Next, evaluate the sales rankings of the top five books. According to Yanik Silver, the ideal ranking is between 5,000 and 150,000. Any lower means not enough people are interested. Too much higher than that means the market is probably oversaturated.[1]

Explore Affiliate Opportunities

Affiliate marketing was explained in chapter 9. Now your mission is to use that information to explore what type of opportunities might exist for each blog. Go to Google and type in your keywords, plus the word *affiliate*. Explore the companies listed to see if they offer products you

Great Blog Topics

- Information—could be a definition or explanation
- Teaching and tips—beyond basic information to how-to instruction
- Quick lists—give the Five Reasons, the Twenty-Five Places, the Ten Mistakes
- Latest news—report about your industry
- Reviews—rate books, movies, products, companies, Web sites
- Resources and links to great sites—become a reliable jumping-off point so people return to your blog when they want to learn about your topic
- Opinion—tell the world what you think!
- Q and A—solicit questions from your readers or create your own list to answer
- Polls and poll results
- Guest commentaries
- Interviews—especially with noted people or experts in your industry
- Profile—write about an influential or intriguing person
- Success stories—if your blog is how-to oriented, tell stories of people who have succeeded by following your advice
- Product comparisons—pick two to five products and compare them with one another
- Pros and cons—give the advantages and disadvantages of a product, service, or approach to a problem
- Trend watch—give your take on recent trends or boldly predict the future

might be interested in selling at some point in the future. Ideally you've picked a topic that offers a wide range of valuable products (some cheap, some expensive) that will pay you a reasonable commission.

> *Ideally you've picked a topic that offers a wide range of valuable products (some cheap, some expensive) that will pay you a reasonable commission.*

Evaluate

Now evaluate. Which of your topics has the highest search rates, the most available products, and the highest potential earning? Of course, be sure to factor in your interest level. Are you truly passionate about the subject? Could you talk about it all day long? Is this a topic you would want to explore in great depth even if you never got paid? If yes, you've made your decision. If not, take another look at one of the other topics on your list. Once you've chosen your blog topic, it's time to launch.

Choose a Hosted or Stand-Alone Blog Platform

Your next decision is whether to choose a hosted or stand-alone blog platform. A platform refers to the specific software you use to create, manage, and broadcast your blog. Your platform is the stage on which you stand to shout your message to the world. Your platform gives you both a center stage (your public place to shine and listen to your cheering fans) and a backstage, typically called a dashboard (where you do all the hard work). Currently, the most popular blogging platforms include Blogger (www.blogger.com) and WordPress (www.wordpress.org or www.wordpress.com).

A hosted blog platform is free, but your potential audience is limited because search engines can't easily find you. For one thing, you aren't permitted to have your own URL (universal resource locator—your home address on the Internet), and it's pretty hard for people to find you when you aren't allowed to have your own address. Instead, your blog is just a small part of the host's enormous blog. For example, Blogger is a free hosted platform. If you sign up with Blogger, your URL will be www.yourname.blogspot.com. WordPress provides both a free hosted version (wordpress.com), as well as a stand-alone version (wordpress.org). If you sign up for the free version, your URL will be www.yourname.wordpress.com. If you get stuck, your domain host should have an 800 number for customer assistance. (For further help with a WordPress blog, visit the affordable tutorial on my Web site—www.makingmoneywithdonna.com/create-a-blog ❈—that walks you step by step through the process of creating your own blog.)

If you're serious about your home business and hope to generate income on the Internet, you should invest in a stand-alone platform so you can have your own address. I recommend WordPress.org. (*Note:* If you decide to go with a free hosted platform, the next section about domains does not apply to you. But read it anyway, because there are other reasons, besides writing a blog, to utilize a domain name.)

Your platform is the stage on which you stand to shout your message to the world.

Stake Your Domain

Congratulations! You're now ready to set up shop along the information superhighway. The first stop is domain registration, which will cost about $10. Your domain is your address or URL. The best choice is almost always ".com" following your name. Incidentally, search your name in Google to see how many other people (if any) have your exact same name. If you get many search results—and you can afford a few extra dollars—you can purchase .net and .org as well.

I have a dear friend in ministry who didn't take this step and discovered that a porn star had the exact same name and took out one of the domains with their shared name. That's an extreme case, but since your name and reputation are a huge part of your future business potential in the blogosphere, it's good to find out these types of things beforehand.

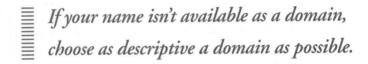

If your name isn't available as a domain, choose as descriptive a domain as possible.

Another friend, who is now a top-selling Christian author, has the same name as a fifteen-year-old girl who "beat her to the net" and purchased the name, which her father tried to resell to my friend for $5,000. Something to think about.

If your name isn't available, choose as descriptive a domain as possible. (For more information concerning domain-registration companies, visit my site, www.makingmoneywithdonna.com/domain, ✳ for my current recommendations.)

Set Up Your E-Mail Account

When you create your domain, you'll see an option to set up free user e-mail accounts. You might want to set up several, including the following:

- yourname@yourdomain.com
- info@yourdomain.com
- affiliates@your domain.com
- comments@yourdomain.com
- yourspouse@yourdomain.com
- anychildrenover12@yourdomain.com

You may or may not need these e-mail accounts, but since they're free, why not set them up just in case? Then if your spouse or children start helping out with the business, they can have their own e-mail associated with your online business. When people want info, they can e-mail specifically to your info address. When you join various affiliate programs, all of the correspondence for those can come into your affiliate e-mail account. This can make things easier to keep track of, but if that sounds too complicated, just create your own name and leave it at that!

The Top Ten Tips for a Great Blog Post

Most people prefer to scan rather than read content on the Internet. They want to be able to quickly get the gist of things. So the trick is to make your blog scan friendly.

1. Write bullet points, not essays.
2. Use headings and subheadings.
3. Include pictures (not family photos, but images related to the topic).
4. Put key points in borders and boxes.
5. Leave white space—don't clutter up the page.
6. Be brief and to the point.
7. Say it up front and then back it up.
8. Stick to one main idea per post.
9. Reinforce and reiterate your points.
10. Include links to other posts on related topics.

(To read some great general-interest blogs, check out the list I've compiled at www.makingmoneywithdonna.com/top-blogs. ✳)

Create and Distribute Your Blog

Once you've set up your blog, you're ready to create content. Take out the list of ten subtopics you made at the beginning of chapter 8. Write out ten things you know about each of those ten subtopics. (See the sidebar "Great Blog Topics" in this chapter.) Now shape those ten points into ten miniarticles. Don't panic when I say miniarticle. Blog posts need to be around 200 to 400 words. Short sentences with small words are best. No one wants to read a college dissertation on the Internet. Think casual, comfortable, and to the point.

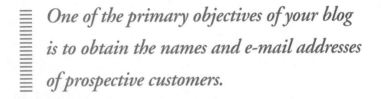

One of the primary objectives of your blog is to obtain the names and e-mail addresses of prospective customers.

You should spend a few days surfing the blogosphere to check out the competition and to see how successful bloggers blog. Turn to your good friend Google to identify the top blogs related to your keywords. That's easy to do. Just type in the keywords plus "blog" and see what turns up. You'll get an excellent idea of how it's done.

Mailing Lists

One of the primary objectives of your blog is to obtain the names and e-mail addresses of prospective customers. You want every person who visits to feel motivated enough to provide you with his or her name, e-mail address, and permission to stay in touch. You can simply invite visitors to sign up for your mailing list, or better yet, make a soft offer. Promise them a free report, access to a downloadable audio, or other valuable information. All they have to do to access it is type in their first name and e-mail address. If you can get people to do that one simple thing, you will lay a fabulous foundation for your home business.

Using an Autoresponder

To manage your mailing list, you'll want to use an autoresponder service. An *autoresponder* is a program that enables you to automatically send a series of e-mails to people once they sign up or opt in to your mailing list. For example, I have an opt-in mailing list for a monthly e-zine. Within seconds of signing up, the person receives an e-mail from me, welcoming them to my circle of friends. Then once a month I send out an e-zine with information, inspiration, invitations to my upcoming events, and special offers in my bookstore.

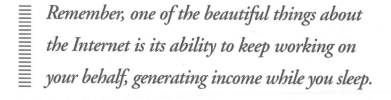

Remember, one of the beautiful things about the Internet is its ability to keep working on your behalf, generating income while you sleep.

You'll want to strike a balance between sending people enough information to demonstrate your knowledge and helpfulness without overwhelming them with information or giving away the store for free. As an example, I created a ninety-day autoresponder to tie in with my previous book *Becoming the Woman I Want to Be*. I promoted it through my Web site as a free support program that encourages greater health and weight loss from the inside out. When people opted in to that list, they immediately received a welcome e-mail, and then every day for the next ninety days, the autoresponder automatically sent them the next message. I set it up once, and then my computer kept in touch with all of these potential customers on my behalf—even while I slept. That's the amazing part! Remember, one of the beautiful things about the Internet is its ability to keep working on your behalf, generating income while you sleep. You may have already guessed one problem with my ninety-day program: It gave too much free help! Why would anyone pay for information from me when I was already giving them, for free, more information than they could effectively process? Although nearly ten thousand people signed up, my program generated very little profit, and a large number of people unsubscribed. Ninety days is just too long to retain interest. Seven to ten follow-up messages is ideal. Then send out a monthly or bimonthly e-zine. (And, of course, I have more help for this topic at www.makingmoneywithdonna.com/autoresponder ✻.)

Get Found—Search-Engine Optimization

Once you've created your first ten blog posts and set up your autoresponder to capture e-mail addresses, you want the search engines to pick up all of your wonderful content and begin driving traffic your way.

The name of the game with blogs is Search-Engine Optimization (SEO). The goal of the game is getting your blog to appear when people sit down at their computers to search for the kind of information you specialize in offering. That's why it's so important to specialize, specialize, specialize! Know who your potential customers are, the kind of questions they will likely ask, and the types of problems they'll need to solve. (See www.makingmoneywithdonna.com/seo ✻.)

Armed with that information and the list of keywords you made earlier, you can shape your blog's content with SEO in mind. The tips in the "Top Ten Search-Engine Optimization Tips" sidebar will help you get found.

Now as you prepare for people to visit your blog, your next step is putting systems in place that will enable you to make money from your blog. That's the topic of later chapters. But first things first, and first is getting known. That's what social networks are for, and we'll cover that in the next chapter.

The Top Ten Search-Engine Optimization Tips

1. **Update your blog every day if you possibly can.** Fresh content is the real king in SEO. (Remember, blog posts need to be only 200 to 400 words.)

2. **Use the keywords your prospective clients will be searching.** Use them in titles and in the content of the blog itself.

3. **Put some keywords in larger, bold fonts.** Don't go crazy, though!

4. **Build relationships with other experts in your field and related areas.** Encourage them to link to your site.

5. **Encourage visitors to post comments on your blog.** Comments count as content.

6. **Use hyphens instead of underscores in your page titles.** For example, "best-baby-formula" instead of "best_baby_formula."

7. **Check your site regularly for broken links.** The quickest and surest way to uncover broken links is by submitting your site to Google analytics. I've created an affordable online tutorial— www.makingmoneywithdonna.com/google-analytics ✱—that walks you through that process.

8. **Actively submit your posts to article directories (see chapter 14).** When you include a link to your blog in every article you put out into cyberspace, those incoming links boost your credibility with search engines.

9. **Install a sitemap on your blog.** See my blog tutorial at www.makingmoneywithdonna.com/create-a-blog ✱.

10. **Link up with search engines.** Take a few moments to submit your blog to the major search engines using the following links:
    - Google (www.google.com/addurl.html)
    - Yahoo (https://siteexplorer.search.yahoo.com/submit)
    - Open Directory (www.dmoz.org/add.html)

Questions ||||||||||||||||||||||||||||||||||||||||||||||||||||||||||||||||||||||||||||||||||||||||||||

1. Which would you like your blog to compare to? Rank in order
    of importance for your business:

    ___ bookstore

    ___ TV or movie studio

    ___ radio station

    ___ photography studio

    ___ retail store

    ___ business

    ___ wholesale distributor

    ___ news outlet

    ___ watercooler

    ___ town hall

    ___ community center

2. List your top-ten potential blog topics.

    _____   _____

    _____   _____

    _____   _____

    _____   _____

    _____   _____

3. What did your keyword search reveal? Which potential blog
    topics seem most promising based on keywords?

4. What did you learn from your Amazon.com book search?

5. Which blog topics had the most promising affiliate opportunities?

6. Did you come up with a clear winner? List your top three.

7. Will you go with a hosted or stand-alone blog platform?

8. Did you stake your domain name? If not, set a specific target date to do so.

9. Have you created your first blog post? If not, set a specific date for doing so.

10. List the top five blogs that turned up in your Google search.

11. What did you like or dislike about each of those blogs?

12. Based on your evaluation in the previous question, what elements will you include in your blog?

ʃocial ∩etworking

Once you've launched your blog and started writing miniarticles related to your business passion, you're ready to begin driving traffic to your location. The cheapest and most effective way to do that is with social networking. In simplistic terms, social networking is the consumer talking back. At the inception of Internet marketing, communication was all one way. Business owners hired professionals to set up Web sites where the company did all the talking, with one goal in mind: selling. Social networking sites have revolutionized the Web by creating a two-way dialogue and a community atmosphere where blatant sales pitches are frowned upon. Now, consumers can tell the large corporations what they want. It's a win-win situation.

Social networking evolves hourly, so this is one area where you'll want to constantly keep on top of trends. (Visit www.makingmoney withdonna.com/social-networking ✳ for current tips.) If you've got something great to offer, the best way to spread the word is no longer with paid advertisements or hard-sell approaches. Those techniques played to the strengths of well-funded corporations while putting the little guys like us at a distinct disadvantage. Today, the best approach is to be personable and helpful, whether you are in a small business or a large one. Think Mary Kay and Starbucks, where personal attention is integrated with the product.

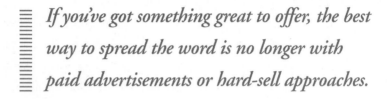

If you've got something great to offer, the best way to spread the word is no longer with paid advertisements or hard-sell approaches.

When people begin to recognize that you actually know your stuff and realize that associating with you is beneficial for them, your influence in the community grows. Similarly, your bank account will grow as your following decides that your products are worth purchasing.

Your objective in social networking is twofold: First, grow friendships to help others succeed. Second, they in turn will help you succeed. This paradigm shift plays directly to the strengths of individual entrepreneurs. All you have to do is be your own wonderful self, sharing your life experiences and expertise from your heart, and the success will take care of itself. This is one of the great benefits of a home-based business— you get paid to be uniquely you.

I'd like to share with you what has worked most effectively for me.

PING.fm

By far my favorite social-media networking tool is Ping.fm. It's a platform that enables you to post to at least forty different social-networking sites, ranging from microblogs like Twitter and Plurk to Facebook and your WordPress blog.

Ping.fm enables you to extend your reach and form connections with the maximum number of people possible. You increase your profile one click at a time. With every friend added on Facebook, every bookmark added to StumbleUpon, or every post entered on Twitter, you become more visible. The higher your profile, the more business will come to you. And that's what Internet marketing via social networks is all about: getting business to come to you.

Go to Ping.fm (http://ping.fm/) and create an account (it's free). Once you get your account, the page will change, and you'll see a long list of places that Ping.fm will post to. For each social network, set up an account (assuming you don't have one yet). A new screen will come

The Top Ten Social-Networking Tips

1. **Be amusing or interesting (or both).** Let your personality shine through. (Again, it all comes back to chapter 5, choosing a topic you find truly fun and enjoyable.)
2. Help people save time and make money.
3. Avoid hard-sell tactics.
4. Offer practical tips that are easily implemented.
5. Share links to good information.
6. **Discussion is great.** Pose interesting questions to promote conversation.
7. **Ask for advice.** People love to feel like they know something you don't.
8. **Find a balance between personal and professional posts.** When you post professionally, be personable. When you post personal stuff, remember you are a professional.
9. **Comment on what others are saying too.** Don't be a one-way communicator. Don't be defensive. Ignore your critics, or better still, be nice to them.
10. **Always wish people a happy birthday.** Facebook makes it easy to do.

up. Create or enter your username and password. Click the boxes to indicate what type of posts you want sent to each network. Follow the same steps for any other sites you belong to that are on the list.

> *The higher your profile, the more business will come to you. And that's what Internet marketing via social networks is all about: getting business to come to you.*

On the Ping.fm home page at the lower right, you'll see a list of services. Click on "Posting By E-mail." (If you can't find it, do a search for that term.) There you'll find your secret posting address. It will include letters followed by "@ping.fm." Put this e-mail into your phone's contacts list as though it were a person. Then whenever you want to post to your social networks, just write an e-mail or send a text message to Ping.fm. Instantly your message will go to your entire network. Instantly! It's amazing! It took me a full weekend to sign up for the various sites, and it was one of the best time investments I've made in a while.

Facebook

My favorite social media site, by far, is Facebook. It's an incredibly fast-growing site where you can network with friends and family as well as everyone in their networks. You can promote live events as well as online events, form interest groups, and more. With hundreds of millions of people and businesses interacting in one place, Facebook is clearly the place to be for the home-based businessperson.

There's currently a distinction between personal Facebook profiles and professional Facebook pages, which are designed for businesses, authors, musicians, and the like. The differences in functionality are moving closer together, and by the time this book is published, all differences may have disappeared. Nevertheless, it's important to know your purpose when you open your Facebook account. Do you want to post pictures of your grandkids to show off in front of your friends? Or are you trying to grow your Internet-based business? If you think the former is a vitally important part of your life, I would strongly encourage you to create two distinct Facebook sites: one personal and one professional.

It's important to know your purpose when you open your Facebook account.

You can post status updates, called microblogging (see the following section), articles (using the Notes feature), pictures, videos, you name it. Facebook is the place to see and be seen.

Twitter

Twitter is a microblogging platform that gives users 140 characters (not words) to answer the question: "What are you doing right now?" It's currently the hottest thing in social media, and it's growing like wildfire. Within my first week on Twitter, I connected with a magazine editor and am now in the process of forming a vital partnership with him.

Doing business on Twitter is tricky because you don't want to be all business, but you don't want to bore people to tears with endless trivia either. A general rule of thumb is to post five personal or generically helpful items for every post that sells you or your product. Personally, I don't care that someone is drinking a Peppermint Mocha Twist at Starbucks, but if he or she comes home to find the dog got into the trash, I might be slightly amused.

Social Bookmarking

Social bookmarking is a way for you to share your favorite sites and information sources with friends and strangers. As you surf the Internet, when you come across something helpful, you "tag" it, making it easier for others to find. In a sense you're voting for content. The more people who tag an article or site, the greater prominence it receives. One of the most popular bookmarking tools is Digg (http://digg.com/), which is also a great tool for submitting your own articles. I've also discovered another great one: ShareThis (www.sharethis.com).

Spamming

Trying to make instant friends with one thousand people with the obvious intent of making a one-way sales pitch is the surest way for social networking to backfire on you. Just as a good word travels fast, so does a bad reputation. Be very, very careful. Social networking can be your

---

Be My Friend

You can start your social networking by becoming my friend on any of the following:

- Digg (http://digg.com/users/donnapartow)
- Facebook (www.facebook.com/donna.partow)
- FriendFeed (http://friendfeed.com/donnapartow)
- LinkedIn (www.linkedin.com/in/donnapartow)
- Plurk (www.plurk.com/user/donnapartow)
- StumbleUpon (http://donnapartow.stumbleupon.com/)
- Twitter (http://twitter.com/donnapartow)
- YouTube (www.youtube.com/donnapartow)

greatest asset or the worst thing that could possibly happen to your business. I'm confident that if you follow the suggestions in this chapter, it will be one of the greatest!

Questions |||||||||||||||||||||||||||||||||||||||||||||||||||||||||||||||||||||||||||||||||||||||||||||||||||||||||||||||

1. What personality traits do you want to convey through social networking?

2. What are some topics related to your business that you can discuss?

3. What are some topics not related to your business but of interest to like-minded people that you can discuss?

4. What ideas do you have for saving time and/or money that can be communicated via social networks?

5. What are some of your favorite Web sites or information sources? You can share links to these via social networks.

Assignments ||||||||||||||||||||||||||||||||||||||||||||||||||||||||||||||||||||||||||||||||||||||||||||||||

1. Go to Facebook.com and create a personal profile.
2. Allow Facebook to search your contact file to instantly link you with friends, family members, and colleagues.
3. Post a photo of yourself. Few things are worse than a faceless Facebook page.
4. Begin posting on your Facebook page. It's fun and easy to do.
5. Search Facebook Groups for any that might be related to your business. Begin joining groups to interact with others and to identify people you can invite as friends, based on mutual interests.
6. If your business is established, create a Facebook fan page. If you're still unclear exactly what your business will entail, hold off on a fan page for now.
7. Go to Ping.fm and set up an account. You can select which social networks you want to connect with from its list.
8. Set up your Twitter page.
9. Send out your first tweet!
10. Begin social bookmarking using ShareThis, Digg, and other sites to make note of interesting articles and information related to your business.

Article Marketing

You've set up your blog. You've selected affiliate products to market. You may even have developed a few original products or joined a direct-selling company so you can offer their products. In other words, the store is open for business. But where will the customers come from? Your blog may be a thing of beauty and a joy forever, but if no one visits it, you're not in business. You're just keeping busy. How do you get people to visit your blog? We've looked at multiple Internet-marketing strategies throughout this book, almost all of which will have relevance for your blog. Let's begin by focusing on one of the top strategies for driving traffic your way: article marketing.

The more information you post along the information superhighway, the easier it is for potential customers to find you. Your articles should be informative and written to benefit the reader. They shouldn't be all about you, but instead they should demonstrate that you know what you're writing about. They should position you as an expert (or the kind of person who knows how to find experts). If an article doesn't deliver quick, usable information, your prospective customer will click away in an instant. That's not what you want to happen. Instead, you want to provide enough help and hope that the reader can tell you have more to offer. He or she will want to click on over to your Web site or blog, where all of your wonderful products and services are just waiting to be evaluated. If you've done a good job, a purchase may occur.

The purpose of article marketing is to get your name out into the blogosphere and position yourself as a leader in your area of expertise. So it's vitally important that every article you write is written with your prospective customer in mind. In other words, if your blog is about breeding and selling dogs, don't write articles about your favorite political candidate. Or if you must do so, use a nom de plume! Some bloggers suggest putting a picture of a typical prospective client above your computer screen, so you can remember the kind of person you're trying to reach. Not a bad idea.

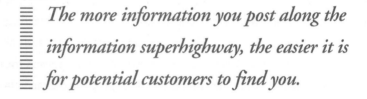

The more information you post along the information superhighway, the easier it is for potential customers to find you.

Think about that person. If she were sitting right in front of you, what questions do you think she would ask? (What questions do you frequently get asked?) What help does she need related to your niche? How can you provide that help? That should be the burning question on your mind during every working hour of the day. If you help people, they will help you pay your bills. That's a fair exchange. You created your blog to provide for your family, and that's a very noble thing. You've spent years developing your expertise (whether it's as a mother or an accountant), and you deserve to be paid for the information you can now provide. I think it's difficult for many women, myself included, to place a value on what we know. But we must learn to do so.

Right next to the photo of your typical prospective customer, put up a family photo as a reminder: You aren't writing articles just to put more information on the blogosphere. You're trying to create a viable business.

What Makes a Great Article?

The following five areas can make or break your article:

1. Captivating title. Your title has a nanosecond to grab the reader's attention. Make sure it reaches out and just about screams: "You've got to read me! I can definitely help you!"

2. Smart use of keywords. The first and last words in the title should be the keywords the person would search for. Let's say you're positioning yourself as an expert on frugality. Your list of keywords probably included coupons. So your article title might be "Coupons: Could You Be Saving Even More with Your Coupons?" Curiosity alone might be enough for someone to click that link, because anyone who cares about coupons wants to find out whether he or she could be saving even more.

3. Solid information. Few things aggravate people more than clicking a link that turns out to be nothing but a sales pitch or a link to a link to a link. I'm sure you've experienced that frustration yourself many times. Do you want any further association with that person or product? Of course not. So pack your article with great information and/or real solutions.

4. Only 300 to 500 words. Although you want to give solid information, people want it fast and to the point. That's why bullet points and checklists work great. Your article doesn't have to be lengthy to be effective. Aim for no more than 300 to 500 words. How do you measure effectiveness? Quite simply by answering this question: Do customers take the next step, which is clicking over to your blog? If so, your article was effective; if not, it wasn't.

5. Form a connection. Your ultimate goal on the Internet is forming connections within the boundaries of business. So after you've shared helpful information, invite readers to get even more information from you. Let them know there's lots more to learn on your blog and that you're committed to helping people just like them solve problems just like the one in the article. This is accomplished with a resource box, which is the most important part of any article. (See the section "Elements of an Effective Resource Box" later in the chapter.)

Why People Search for Information on the Internet

Remember that people search the Internet for two primary reasons: to get answers to their questions and to find solutions to their problems. So your mission is to create content that answers questions and solves problems. Pretty simple, right? Therefore, the simplest and most effective approach to article marketing is creating articles that pose questions (then provide answers) or present problems (then solve them). The following is an explanation of how to write an article that does both.

Articles that Answer a Question

People are drawn to titles that pose a question and, by implication, promise the answer they're looking for. They also want specificity. In particular, people like numbers—3 Ways, 5 Reasons, 10 Surefire Strategies, and so on. You can use those two factors to craft articles that will draw and hold readers' attention. So create a catchy title like this:

"Are You Making the 5 Most Common _____ Mistakes _____ Make?"

Your target might be golfers, homeschooling moms, grandparents, people trying to lose weight, teachers, runners, whatever! Fill in the category in the article title with a specific topic and a description of your target audience.

Let's use the example of homeschooling moms. Now, because you're limited to just 300 to 500 words, you couldn't possibly tackle every conceivable mistake on every related topic. So let's narrow it down to marriage mistakes that homeschooling moms make: "Homeschooling Moms—Are You Making the 5 Most Common Marriage Mistakes Homeschooling Moms Make?"

Next, make a list of the five most common marriage mistakes you think homeschoolers make:

1. Becoming too child focused
2. Neglecting romance
3. Neglecting personal appearance
4. Neglecting household upkeep
5. Nagging the spouse to be more involved

Write a sentence or two about each mistake, how easy it is for people to make it, and the negative consequences of the mistake. Now the reader knows you understand her problems. All that remains is to position yourself as someone who has the solutions the reader is looking for. You are the expert. So next describe how you handle each of these situations to prevent making those common mistakes. Make sure your solutions are practical and can be easily put into action. If you effectively do so, you may have just won over a potential customer.

> *All that remains is to position yourself as someone who has the solutions the reader is looking for. You are the expert.*

Last, but most important, call for action. What do you want the reader to do? The most obvious is to send for your free special report. That way you capture an e-mail address and can add this person to your list of future customers.

Generating More Articles

Once you've written an article on common marriage mistakes home-schooling moms make, you can tackle other common mistakes home-schooling moms make and turn each of those into articles as well:

- Trying to re-create a classroom environment in the home
- Going to homeschool conventions without a strategy or preset budget
- Not following a tight enough schedule . . . or being too rigid
- Failing to find the right balance of outside activities for the children
- Neglecting self-care

You can see how quickly you can produce twenty-five articles. Every article begins the same way. Start by listing common problems or pit-falls related to your niche. Make a list of ways to avoid the problem or solve the problem, or on the positive side, ways to do whatever it is bet-ter. If you're a homeschooling mom, I guarantee you could write 300 to 500 words about all of the above. It's so much easier than you think.

An Article a Day?

Experts in the field of article marketing suggest you write and post an article a day. This sounds a bit overwhelming, even to me as a profes-sional writer. Perhaps two days per week is a more reasonable goal. But if you become proficient, it shouldn't take more than sixty to ninety minutes to create and post a 300-word article. Just remember that the more articles you produce, the more people you help, the more traffic you drive to your blog, and the more money you make.

Focus on helping people, and if you create enough information products for those people to purchase from you, they can help you in return by compensating you for the years you've spent acquiring enough wisdom to become an expert on your topic.

Article Directories

What do you do with your article once you've written it? Obviously, you can post it on your blog. You can gather a collection of articles and send them out as part of a weekly or monthly e-zine. But since the real purpose of article marketing is drawing in new people who don't already read your blog and haven't already subscribed to your mailing list, the place to be is in article directories.

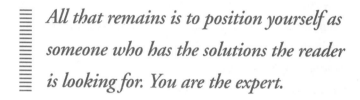

All that remains is to position yourself as someone who has the solutions the reader is looking for. You are the expert.

An article directory brings together people who create content (authors, bloggers, etc.) with those who need content (publishers). As a content creator, you join free and post your articles for individuals to read and publishers to publish for yet more people to read your brilliant thoughts. Everyone wins . . . especially you, if you learn to do it right.

E-zineArticles

One of the top article-directory sites is EzineArticles (http://ezinearticles.com/). This one site receives more than 15 million unique views a month, according to current Internet reviews. A great feature about this Web site is that when you post your article, the system automatically notifies thousands of publishers who have specifically requested content on your topic. In addition, they'll send an update with your article title directly to your Twitter home page. This expands your reach to everyone in your Twitter circle of influence.

As you can see, article marketing is a powerful and free pathway toward making money from home. All you need is belief in yourself and a commitment to spend an hour a day, three to five days per week writing down solutions to problems you've been solving for years. The difference is that now you might get paid for all your hard-won wisdom and knowledge.

Here are some other article directories worth checking out:

- GoArticles (www.goarticles.com)
- Web Source (www.web-source.net)
- Article Alley (www.articlealley.com)
- Buzzle.com (www.buzzle.com)
- SubmitYOURArticle.com (www.submityourarticle.com)

Elements of an Effective Resource Box

The last paragraph of every article you write should include what's called a *resource box*. It's not really a box; it's just the last paragraph in every article you submit anywhere on the Internet. In it you let readers know that you have more resources related to the topic they've just read about. If they found your information helpful, they'll take up your offer to come to you to learn even more. Take this opportunity to record their e-mail addresses so you can keep in touch with them and hopefully turn all of those article readers into actual paying customers.

Your resource box must include the following:

- your name
- your business name
- your microbio—why you're qualified to write the article, and why the reader should look to you for further information
- your full URL (for example, http://www.yourname.com)
- a free offer

The last sentence of every article should begin with a phrase like "And now I'd like to invite you . . . ," "And now I'd like to offer you . . . ," or "Claim your free instant access to . . . ," followed by a brief description of a helpful in-depth article, minireport, audio, or video you offer.

The Top Ten Article-Marketing Tips

1. **Research your subject an hour a day so you stay current.** Read blogs, subscribe to podcasts, and attend teleseminars and live conferences in your field of interest. Become a genuine expert.

2. **Write twenty headlines for every potential article.** Choose the one that clearly targets your audience and promises a powerful benefit.

3. **Write short, pithy, power-packed articles with lots of bullets.**

4. **Share valuable information and resources in every article.** Make sure everything you post has solid takeaway value; don't post fluff and nonsense. Respect your readers' time, and you'll win their respect. Waste their time, and you'll lose their respect.

5. **Register at five or more article directory sites.**

6. **Post at least one article per week.**

7. **Post your articles on Twitter, Facebook, and other social-networking sites.** Use Ping.fm as your one-stop platform.

8. **Include links to other related articles you've written within each article.** These links should take the reader to your blog, where you've posted all your prior articles.

9. **Make sure your resource box is as effective as possible.** Test different approaches and see which draws the best response.

10. **Recycle your articles into information products.** Once you've written twenty great articles on a topic, compile them into a special report and sell it for $7.50. Fifty or more articles would make a great e-book to sell for $17 or more. Or you might add in a weekly teleseminar and turn your articles into the foundation of an e-course for $27, $47, or even $97, depending upon the content.

Include a direct link to your blog, where the information is stored. To access the information, the reader should be required to give you his or her first name and e-mail address.

Don't make the mistake of requiring more information from customers than you truly need, because (1) people are too busy to bother, and (2) people dislike giving out too much personal data on the Internet, with good reason. (We discussed this in the "Free Information" section in chapter 8.)

Questions ||||||||||||||||||||||||||||||||||||||||||||||||||||||||||||||||||||||||||||||||||||||||||||||||||||||||||||

1. How many days per week can you set aside an hour to research and write an article to further your goal of making money from home?

2. Which days? What time? Commit and schedule it.

3. Did you investigate article directories? Did you register at EzineArticles.com? If not, commit to a certain date when you will do so.

4. When do you plan to post your first article? Let the deadline drive you to productivity.

Assignments |||||||||||||||||||||||||||||||||||||||||||||||||||||||||||||||||||||||||||||||||||||||||||||||

1. List at least ten article topics.

   _____   _____

   _____   _____

   _____   _____

   _____   _____

   _____   _____

2. On a separate sheet of paper, brainstorm twenty potential headlines for each of the ten articles. Choose the most potent.

3. Write the proposed text for your resource box.

Strategies to Keep Your Business Growing

Your home-based business will succeed or fail depending upon how effectively you market. You may offer the greatest product or service in the history of the world, but if no one has ever heard of you, you won't be in business very long.

Now we get to the high-hurdles portion of our program! Who taught you to conduct market research? Target an audience? Develop a "unique selling proposition"? Deliver a can't-miss sales presentation? No one? That's no surprise. Our educational system deliberately trains people to become employees, not entrepreneurs. Now you can sit around bemoaning that fact, or you can become a self-taught marketing maniac.

Marketing may sound like a complex subject, but it's actually quite simple. Any communication between you and a potential customer is marketing. Once you overcome your fear of rejection, marketing might even become fun! This chapter will review the top ten conventional marketing strategies.

Develop a Unique Selling Proposition (USP)

Get this one right, and the rest of your marketing will be a breeze. Well, almost. Come up with a totally unique product or service—or just a unique delivery system (Dell offered the first mail-order computers) or unique style (Mary Kay's pink Cadillacs). Deliver superior quality with a novel, even unconventional, twist, and people may well buy just because they remember you. Whatever it takes!

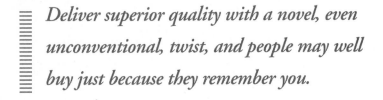

Deliver superior quality with a novel, even unconventional, twist, and people may well buy just because they remember you.

One of the biggest mistakes people make when they start making money from home is deciding that their unique selling proposition is "I'm the cheapest." That's not a USP! Stop and think. Do you really want people to buy your products just because they're the cheapest? How will you feel providing a service to someone who hired you only because he thought he was getting a bargain? Cheaper is not always better. In fact, when it comes to home businesses, I'd say cheaper is almost always worse. You don't need to be cheap; you need to be unique.

Charlie Dunn worked on an assembly line stitching boots for little better than minimum wage. Eventually those boots made their way into stores, where they sold for about $100 a pair. But one day he looked in the mirror and decided he was worth more. So he launched his own business making customized boots by hand. Did he sell his boots for $50? Not on your life. He made boots to sell for thousands of dollars per pair. He made boots for Ronald Reagan, Clint Eastwood, even the pope.

Country-western star Jerry Jeff Walker loved Charlie's boots so much, he wrote a song about them.

Same man. Same product. What made the difference? He set his sights not on being the cheapest but on being the best. He had a USP: one-of-a-kind handmade boots. I'd say that's unique.

How about you? As you consider what your products or services are worth, will you settle for being cheaper? Or will you dare to be unique?

How to Price a Product

Too many home-business owners don't pay themselves a decent wage. Don't make that mistake. Instead, use the following formula to establish a fair price:

1. Decide on the *minimum* wage you're willing to work for:

   _____

2. Determine the amount of time invested in each product:

   _____

3. Calculate your material costs: _____

4. The minimum price you need to charge is (#1 x #2) + #3.

5. Evaluate the market. Can you get your price? If not, don't lower the price. Instead, choose another product.

Let me give you an example:

1. You're willing to work for $8 per hour.

2. It takes you five hours to make each product.

3. Your materials cost $20.

4. The minimum price you would have to charge is: $8 x 5 hours = $40 for time; then you add the material costs ($20) for a total of $65.

Pursue Tie-Ins

A new business owner's toughest obstacle is overcoming suspicion. People don't trust strangers, and that's what you are until your business is well established. To overcome this obstacle and gain instant credibility, tie in with a respected larger business. For example, I have tied in my Home Business Workshop with the CIA (yep, the CIA!), senators, governors, and various Christian organizations. They market the event under their name, thus attracting a larger audience. In some cases I was paid a set fee; other times I received a per-attendee price. On other occasions I agreed to share whatever profit the event generated. Even though I had to share the profits, I still came out ahead because there was a lot more to share.

Whom can you tie in with? Make a list of every product or service that might be related to your business in some way. For example, if you make wedding cakes, think of photographers, videographers, caterers, florists, and so on. Now spend every working minute you possibly can taking samples of your wedding cake to people in those related businesses. Form strategic partnerships that create a win-win for all involved.

How to Price a Service

Asking price equals perceived value. Too many home-business owners undercharge, hoping to gain a competitive advantage. It'll never work. Charge what you're worth and be worth what you charge. Research the annual salary for an employee performing comparable work. Then add on your estimated operating expenses for the year. Divide the total by fifty weeks per year, then by forty hours per week. That's how much you need to pay yourself. But since you won't be able to bill every hour you work, charge your client at least twice that amount.

Send Out Press Releases

Write one- to two-page articles about your business and send them to magazines and newspapers read by your target audience. Many articles are based on press releases; of those, I'd bet half run them word for word. Newsworthy topics include commenting on trends, offering practical tips, or announcing start-up and business anniversaries, major clients landed, and upcoming speeches or seminars.

As of this writing the print-publishing industry is in the midst of an upheaval. *Reader's Digest* filed for bankruptcy in 2009. Recently a major newspaper went out of business after 150 years. Magazines are turning off the presses and becoming e-zines instead. This presents two opportunities for you. First, budget cuts will force print publications to rely more heavily on press releases like yours. And as we've seen, any shift away from expensive advertising wars toward publishing on the Internet is a shift in favor of home-business marketers.

Plant Seeds

The cheapest and most effective marketing is accomplished by word of mouth—and some mouths are worth more than others! Who are the trendsetters, opinion shapers, authorities, and celebrities in your industry—folks like magazine and newspaper columnists, radio and TV hosts, club presidents, and civic leaders? Identify individuals who can authoritatively spread the word, and then plant a seed by giving them a free taste of your business. Plant your seeds and then watch them grow! The more seeds you plant, the greater the harvest.

For example, my publisher will send free copies of this book to every Christian magazine editor, radio, and television-show producer, as well as many influential women's-ministry leaders. If these potential influencers like the book and recommend it to others, I'm in business! The publisher understands that each book it gives away for free to an influencer has the potential to yield a thousandfold—and even more.

Give Speeches and Seminars

One of the most valuable skills a home-business owner can possess is the ability to speak up for her business. Whether you're making a one-on-one presentation to a potential client, offering seminars to promote your business, or speaking to the local Rotary club to get your name out, the ability to state your case persuasively is absolutely crucial. The surest route to home-business success is establishing yourself as an expert or leader in your field. Once you've done so, the onerous task of marketing becomes simple. Business will come to you.

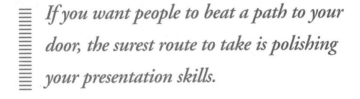

If you want people to beat a path to your door, the surest route to take is polishing your presentation skills.

If you want people to beat a path to your door, the surest route to take is polishing your presentation skills. You can then parlay those skills into information products that cost virtually nothing to develop but yield rich dividends. This is the information age. It doesn't matter if your primary business involves a product or a service; information products can enhance your bottom line with minimal investment. Among those information products might be a full-day seminar, a half-hour presentation, audiocassettes, even a self-published book or booklet transcribed from taped presentations.

Another bonus of learning to speak up for your business is that once you are skilled enough, you actually get paid to market yourself. That's right! Organizations will pay you to talk to audiences filled with your potential customers. When it comes time for these prospective clients to decide whose product or service to buy, whom do you think they'll choose? The guy sitting next to them . . . or the person behind the microphone? The answer is obvious.

So don't just sit there all alone in your home office. Get out there and speak up for your business. Toastmasters International (www.toast masters.org) is the world's largest organization devoted to communication excellence. Through local clubs, Toastmasters offers you the opportunity to learn—and practice—speaking skills. Clubs meet weekly and are located in most communities in America.

Now I earn more money through paid speaking engagements than I do from book sales or any other business endeavor.

Once you've gained some confidence at your local Toastmasters, contact local adult education programs in your area and indicate your availability and credentials to present workshops and seminars. You might also offer to speak for local churches and community groups— free of charge, if necessary. Remember, in these contexts, you'll be selling yourself and your knowledge, not necessarily your product or service. But you'll receive exposure and the hope for future business.

When I was first getting started, I made a phone call to the local school district's continuing-education program and indicated my availability to conduct evening workshops on working at home. As it turned out, district administrators were very interested. I taught several classes, enabling me to earn a respectable hourly income while providing me with additional exposure to the community. Now I earn more money through paid speaking engagements than I do from book sales or any other business endeavor.

Get Booked on Radio and TV Shows

More than one thousand shows require one million guests per year. The opportunities are incredible! There's a whole lot of air time to fill, so why not wax eloquent about your industry? While on the air, be sure to mention your free special report, available through your Web site. This is a great way to drive traffic to your Web site and, if you do it correctly, build your mailing list for future sales.

Getting on *Good Morning America* may be beyond your reach, but local television and radio stations run talk shows on a daily basis. Did you ever stop to think where they find guests day after day? How are those guests selected? Station managers, or other staff, are paid to find experts in various fields and other interesting people. Just think what a great favor you'll be doing them by offering to lend your presence to their show. If you have something interesting to say and are able to express yourself well, go for it!

Radio talk shows present an excellent opportunity for you to promote your home-based business, whether you market a product or serve as a consultant. "Fifteen minutes on the radio revolutionized my business," says Rhonda Anderson of St. Cloud, Minnesota, founder of Creative Memories. She is referring to her appearance on Focus on the Family, one of America's most recognized Christian radio programs with two thousand outlets in the United States. Rhonda goes on to say,

> I knew the show reached my target audience—homemakers. So I hoped to generate interest in my program. It took five months of letters and phone calls—and a personal visit to the show's producer—before I finally got on the program. My efforts were

well rewarded, though. As a direct result of the program, we received more than seven thousand calls and recruited six hundred women.

Today her modest home business has become a multimillion-dollar business.

As we saw in chapter 8 in the section on "Audio Information Products," you can also appear on Internet radio shows and easily launch your own Internet radio show as well.

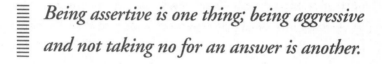

Being assertive is one thing; being aggressive and not taking no for an answer is another.

A note of caution: You can be your own worst enemy and easily damage your reputation and your business if you cold call and insist on talking to everyone in the organization to try to get on a show or in a magazine, get your book published, or whatever you're trying to do. Being assertive is one thing; being aggressive and not taking no for an answer is another. If a producer or editor says your product isn't right for the organization/publisher/show, accept it gracefully. There are other shows and publishers, and there will be other opportunities. Do your homework and determine which shows are the best fit before approaching any of them. And always be sure to go through the proper channels; don't try to do an end run.

Network

Cultivate contacts for personal support, information, professional advice, referrals, and of course, new business. Networking involves making specific plans to meet people who can provide you with personal and professional support, useful information, and business. When you think of establishing a network, first look to your current circle of friends and business associates. Many of them probably can and will be of service in numerous ways. Perhaps your cousin Bob is a computer salesman. He can give you advice and, hopefully, a great discount. Your former boss might be willing to hire you as a subcontractor or consultant. Maybe your next-door neighbor is on the staff of the local newspaper; she may help you get some publicity.

Another note of caution: Many of us have been the recipients of pressurized sales pitches cloaked as "hospitality." This is usually the tactic of the "friends" who offer an invitation to dinner only to coerce you to join their multilevel marketing business. That's a fast way to make people feel used. Networking is a legitimate way to build business contacts, but don't abuse your friends and relatives by thinking of them only in terms of business and always turning hospitality into a business function. Again, don't pester friends, relatives, or neighbors. Offer them your product or service, let them know about special deals or opportunities when appropriate, but don't turn every encounter into a sales pitch or pressure people to buy or to further your business concerns. You don't want them to run the other way when they see you coming!

Your Current Contacts Are, More Than Likely, Not Sufficient

Like it or not, when it comes to business, who you know is often more important than what you know. So try to get to know as many people as possible. Consider joining local and/or national organizations, such as the chamber of commerce. Attend seminars and workshops geared to small-business owners or others who may be able to use your service or product.

Trade associations—such as the American Bar Association, the National Association of Business Support Services (formerly the National Association of Secretarial Services), and hundreds of others— exist for many fields. There's bound to be one related to your business. Joining will give you the opportunity to meet people who have faced similar struggles and can provide valuable advice.

> *Like it or not, when it comes to business, who you know is often more important than what you know. So try to get to know as many people as possible.*

Wherever you go, be sure to carry business cards and hand them out liberally. These are small enough that most people are willing to save them, whereas they might toss a brochure or advertisement. And be sure to ask for business cards from people who might be future business associates. Immediately transfer the information into your business phone, computer, or both. You may even find that elusive but desirable individual known as a mentor. That's someone who not only has been down the road you're traveling but is also willing to share experiences and help you along the way.

Win Over Your Most Important Customer

The most important customer you will ever win is . . . you. That's because enthusiasm is an emotion, and emotions are absolutely contagious. Think about it: When people start hooting and hollering for the home team, normally low-key people join in with abandon. When someone starts laughing uncontrollably, few people in the room can resist joining in. When someone cries from the heart, those around that person are often moved to tears.

Nothing can replace an enthusiastic belief in your business, the kind of belief that can't be shaken or defeated by set-backs. That's because beliefs shape our emotions and emotions are contagious. Think about it. When one person laughs, others in the room naturally begin laughing. If someone begins to cry, others are often moved to tears. If your dominant emotion is fear, people pick up on that and are afraid to buy from you. If you are dominated by doubt, others will doubt you as well. But if you are sincerely confident that you have something of value to offer, and you genuinely care about people, that positive emotion will also be contagious. Since buying is an emotional decision (never a logical one—instead we use logic to justify the emotional purchase), maintain a close watch over your emotions when you interact with prospects and clients.

As I always say: *Believe in you, and others will too.* Keep that thought foremost in your mind as you set out to launch your own business.

Constantly Study Marketing

You should read everything you can get your hands on about marketing! Attend seminars—both live and online. Constantly strive to learn and grow. As I mentioned earlier, one reason I recommend partnering with a direct-sales company for at least one of your businesses is that they constantly provide sales training and professional-development opportunities. If you do nothing else but use the products personally and study marketing, it's worth the price of admission. The best books on marketing for the home-based business owner include anything in the Guerrilla Marketing series by Jay Conrad Levinson. Also take advan-

tage of online marketing seminars. You'll find a current listing of recommended marketing-training resources at www.makingmoneywith
donna.com/marketing.

Questions |||||||||||||||||||||||||||||||||||||||||||||||||||||||||||||||||||||||||||||||||||||||||||||||||

1. What's unique about you?

2. What's unique about the product or service you plan to
   offer?

3. What price range do you want to target in your market—low,
   middle, or high end? Why?

4. Who can you "seed" products or services to?

5. What are some ways you can begin to position yourself as an expert in your field?

6. Who, in your existing circle of influence, can you begin networking with?

Assignments ||||||||||||||||||||||||||||||||||||||||||||||||||||||||||||||||||||||||||||||||||||||||||

1. Write out your unique selling proposition (USP).

2. Use the formulas in this chapter to begin setting prices for your products and/or services. Make a list of every product or service that might be related to your business in some way.

_____   _____

_____   _____

_____   _____

_____   _____

_____   _____

_____   _____

_____   _____

_____   _____

3. Contact individuals, corporations, and organizations that offer those types of products or services to discuss potential tie-in opportunities.

4. Write and send your first press release.

5. Begin seeding your product or service to influential people.

6. Join Toastmasters to hone your speaking skills.

7. Begin developing speaking topics. Jot down your ideas.

8. When you're ready to begin speaking on your topic, contact local churches or organizations that routinely require guest speakers.

9. Contact radio and TV programs about guest opportunities.

10. Develop a networking strategy that includes your existing circle of influence and then extends to local business networks and associations.

11. If you haven't done so already, you need to have business cards created at this time.

Part V

‖‖

Family First

How do veteran home-based business owners keep going? To find out, take a look at Deanna Allen, who knows how to juggle family, business, and fun.

Deanna is the mother of five children; one is in college and four are homeschooled, ages fourteen, eight, six, and four. She left corporate America nine years ago and hasn't looked back. She recalls, "I didn't want to be a slave to someone else's agenda, but I also didn't want to be an irresponsible employee, calling in all the time because my children needed me."

Deanna's first business endeavor was real estate, something she continues to this day as one of her multiple streams of income. In cooperation with an exceptional team of real-estate agents in Northern California and a variety of industry professionals, she is able to do everything from buying and selling to negotiating short sales and foreclosures.

She also serves as property manager for the half-dozen single-family residences she co-owns with her husband; this brings in steady rental income.

In addition to her real-estate business, she earns a modest monthly income as national director of Daughters of Destiny, the fastest-growing women's prison ministry in the country under the nonprofit Impact for Life Ministries. Although she handles all of the administrative work from her home in California, she travels to the ministry headquarters in Colorado and visits prisons nationwide. Deanna also has a growing speaking ministry beyond prison walls and is the author of several Christian books.

"I didn't want to be a slave to someone else's agenda, but I also didn't want to be an irresponsible employee, calling in all the time because my children needed me."

Rounding out her multiple streams of income, she is a distributor for a health-and-wellness network-marketing business.

So how does she juggle it all? "Laser-focused chunks of time," she anwers. "That's my secret." Deanna lives by her calendar. Actually, three calendars: her computerized calendar on Microsoft Outlook, a giant wall calendar, and a day planner into which she inserts daily printouts from her Outlook calendar. She uses a color-coded self-management system that she considers "piecemealed from Franklin Covey and other self-management gurus."

"The color coding enables me to see at a glance if I'm getting out of balance," Deanna explains. "I routinely ask myself questions like these: Am I spending too much time on business? Am I allowing enough time for homeschooling and family? If not, I take out my colored highlighter and mark off a chunk of family time."

Laser-focused chunks of time mean that when she's with her family, she's totally focused on her family. She's not checking e-mail; she doesn't answer the phone. It also means when she's conducting business, her family must respect that as well. In fact, she has specific times of day to do business tasks. "I return calls between 10:30 and 11:30 AM and then again between 4:00 and 5:00 PM, and that's it. I'm not on the phone all day." She also checks e-mail at set times during the day.

Deanna is a big fan of Microsoft Outlook. "Besides the color coding, I love the Share feature, which enables my husband to access my calendar and add items to it. In consultation with him, I plan my week; then I print out my plans and snap the page into my planner, and I'm ready to go." Deanna agreed to share her color system with us. Perhaps you can adapt it for your own family-and-business juggling act:

- Purple—family
- Yellow—nonprofit out-of-state activities
- Orange—nonprofit administrative work from home
- Green—all other income-generating activity (property management, speaking engagements, real estate, network marketing)
- Blue—personal time (Bible study, exercise, girl time)
- Fuchsia—birthdays and special events to remember

Even with this elaborate system, Deanna advises, "Organize your life but stay flexible. Flexible people don't break. Find the balance between being flaky and being driven; between too much and too little time spent on your business. A happy home life gives me the energy to pursue my business endeavors. When our homes are out of balance, everything suffers. Everything feels like a negative pull. What we used to enjoy, now we feel resentful about, and no one can be successful in that negative energy."

Planning meals ahead of time, cooking ahead on Saturdays, and learning to make use of a Crock-Pot are just a few of the strategies that help Deanna manage the demands on her time. She also keeps plenty of healthy snacks like fruits, munchable veggies, and granola on hand for the kids to grab when they're hungry.

> *"Organize your life but stay flexible.*
> *Flexible people don't break."*

As I mentioned earlier, another key for someone who has children at home is getting them involved in the business from an early age. Deanna agrees. "I sit my children down at the table and let them fold newsletters and put postage on envelopes. When boxes arrive, I let the children open them and put things on the shelves. When they're involved, they have a stake in the success of the venture. You never want them to feel resentful."

Deanna learned that strategy from her own mother, who also worked from home. "She had a beauty shop and sold Amway products. So, really, I began working from home at age twelve. I often say, 'I was trained, not raised' and now I'm doing the same for my children. I'm a big fan of delegating and giving children age-appropriate responsibilities. Otherwise I'd go insane."

This busy work-from-home mom also takes time for herself. "I've got to have my daily time with my heavenly Father. That's first. But I also enjoy taking a walk, a hot bath, or a nap. Mommy has to take care of Mommy."

Balancing the Needs of Your Children and Your Business

There are many reasons for deciding to work from home. Often a parent wants to spend more time with young children, or the cost of day care makes working outside the home unfeasible. Some parents decide that their teens need more supervision. Many individuals and couples are caring for elderly parents or a family member who is disabled. For others, downsizing has put an end to an in-house job and made working from home a necessity.

Unless you live alone, you'll need to consider the needs of your family members—even if it's just you and your spouse. Families come in many different configurations, and most of them require a balancing act. In addition to those with children or elderly parents in the home, there are the special circumstances of single parents, empty nesters, or those who are married but have never had children, and those with spouses who travel or work out of town.

Whatever your situation, if your plans for making money from home are going to thrive, you'll need to learn the delicate art of balancing the needs of your family and your business. This chapter includes a wide range of strategies to enable you to do just that. Depending on your family situation, some of the ideas will work, while others may not. Experiment with several options, invent your own, and find out how others who work at home are managing.

Involving Your Children in Your Business

As your children watch you carry out the daily tasks of your business, they'll come to respect you as a businessperson and as someone whose whole world doesn't revolve solely around them. Believe it or not, being the center of their parents' world is a heavy load for children to carry. They want Mom to have a life of her own.

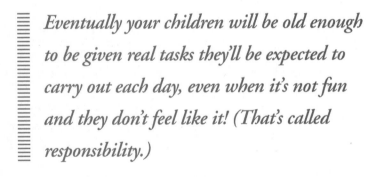

Eventually your children will be old enough to be given real tasks they'll be expected to carry out each day, even when it's not fun and they don't feel like it! (That's called responsibility.)

Even at the youngest age, your children are learning just by watching you. Soon they want to be involved once in a while just because it seems fun. Don't brush aside their offers to assist. Let them make messes and mistakes! Eventually they'll be old enough to be given real tasks they'll be expected to carry out each day, even when it's not fun and they don't feel like it! (That's called responsibility.) As they grow in skill, you can pay them for their work. Let them learn and grow with you.

The Top Ten Ways to Balance Parenting and Your Business

1. **Establish office hours.** It's wise to set aside a specific time each day to work. During that time, post a Mom [or Dad] Working sign and instruct the children to play quietly, read, draw, or color. You might let the kids have their own office space, where they can work while you do. Give them paper, crayons, scissors, or if possible, scrap material related to your business, and let them have their own projects just like you.

   Be sure to establish a tradition of coffee breaks so the kids can look forward to a special time with you. They'll be less likely to interrupt if they know that at 10:30 you always spend a half hour with them.

2. **Work the night shift.** After your spouse comes home from work, he can take the kids for bike rides, play games, read stories, and give them their nightly bath while you work. (However, make sure you later have Daddy and Mommy time, too!)

3. **Understand that your children's sleep time equals your work time.** Many women with small ventures find that simply staying up late or waking up early, plus working during naps, provides enough time for a home business. Remember, you can't force your children to sleep during nap time, but you can require them to lie quietly on their beds.

4. **Get some work-time toys.** Purchase special toys or DVDs that can be used only while Mom works.

5. **Use the TV wisely.** Of course, TV should never be used as a babysitter, but once in a while, quality TV is okay. Perhaps you

can let your youngsters watch public television each morning while you work.

6. **Create a chore chart.** Developing a chore chart is advisable
for all mothers, but it's mandatory for mothers with home
businesses. The children can be encouraged to work on
their chores during your office hours. In addition to household duties, assign your children jobs related to your home
business. When my youngest daughter wakes up each day,
she checks her whiteboard to get her daily assignments
and marks them off as they are completed. (See Dr. James
Dobson's book *The New Dare to Discipline* for further details
on assigning chores.)

7. **Utilize sibling care.** If you have both preschool and school-age
children, the older children can entertain the younger ones for
a period of time each day. You might reward them with a special treat or extra allowance for helping in this way. Let your
kids know that playtime's a-comin'. In order for your children to
understand your need to work, you need to understand their
need to play. So take frequent hug-and-fun breaks, and have
set times when you put business aside and just flat-out play.

8. **Enlist friends and relatives.** If Grandma thinks it's important
for her grandchildren to have a mother at home, ask her to
pitch in with some practical help. Even if she can take your
children one or two mornings a week, you'll be amazed how
much you can get accomplished without distractions. If you
have friends or relatives nearby, particularly with children
close in age to your own, they may be willing to help out
from time to time. They may agree to watch your children,
especially if you can get them excited about your business.

9. **Form playgroups or organize a babysitting co-op.** I belonged to a weekly playgroup with eight other moms, so my turn to host rolled around once every other month. On the other seven Thursday mornings, I got two and a half hours of working time while my daughters enjoyed playing with their favorite friends. And it was free!

   I also belonged to a babysitting co-op with thirty women. To get started, each member paid $5. In return, they received twenty laminated coupons, each worth a half hour of free babysitting, plus a list of all the other members. When I needed a sitter so I could concentrate on my work, I simply called another mom.

   Or you can set up a babysitting exchange. An alternative to a large group is for two home-business moms to alternate care each week. One Friday you entertain the children at your house while your friend works at home. The next week it's her turn. I know a number of women who use this approach successfully.

10. **Hire a mother's helper.** You can hire a preadolescent or teenage girl to play with your children while you work. Since you're in the home, you can hire girls as young as ten to play with your preschoolers. Frankly I've found that the younger girls are much more fun! If your business becomes extremely successful, you can even hire a full-time nanny. Why not think big?

    (For additional strategies and ideas, including how to form playgroups and mother's cooperatives, check out my e-book *Thriving—Not Just Surviving—As a Stay-at-Home Mom*, available at www.makingmoneywithdonna.com/thriving).

I started my home business when I was pregnant with my daughter Leah, who is now nineteen. So she literally grew up with the business, and I've watched her grow along with me: from watching Mommy from her playpen perspective, to stuffing and licking envelopes, to coloring pictures to sell at my book table, to processing credit-card orders (and earning a percentage for each one). Taraneh, (now thirteen) had her first paid speaking engagement by age twelve. She already has her own checking account and earns money making and selling bookmarks at my events.

As your children watch you carry out the daily tasks of your business, they'll come to respect you as a businessperson and as someone whose whole world doesn't revolve solely around them.

Training Your Children for the Future

Having participated in your business, your children will have a greater knowledge of the business world. They'll also be able to avoid the catch-22 most young people face when they're first starting out on their own: They can't get a job without experience, and they can't get experience without a job.

My daughter Leah graduated from high school with an impressive résumé of accomplishments, including operating a very profitable jewelry business and organizing a teen conference that attracted seven hundred teens and adults.

By assisting you with your business, your children will also learn the value of a dollar, and they'll better appreciate when their needs are provided for, not by some mysterious paycheck, but as a direct result of money they've watched you earn by the sweat of your brow. My own sense is that my children have far greater respect for my work than they would if I simply vanished to some mysterious office each day.

If your business becomes successful or particularly enjoyable to your children, you may even pass it along to them as an inheritance. Whether

---

Compensation Strategies

There are a variety of ways to compensate your children for their help with your business. Here's an overview:

- **Hourly wage.** Obviously, this is the only appropriate method for paying an adult child, but you can also pay children and teens an hourly wage.
- **Allowance.** If your business is based at home, you can require your children to fulfill certain duties to help with the business as part of their overall chores. In return, they'd receive a fixed weekly allowance.
- **Volunteer.** This is for you big meanies out there! Yes, we did interview some folks who expected their children to work for the family business *because it was the family business.* Since the business puts food on the table and the children like to eat, they should be willing to work. We think this is a bit cruel . . . but it's an option!

I'd recommend going ahead and putting your kids on your home-business payroll. Since they're in a lower tax bracket, it's a perfectly legitimate way to save on your taxes. However, once your children turn eighteen, they'll be taxed at the same rate as the rest of us.

or not you decide to employ your children, remember to love them, and not just in words. Love them enough to keep them first and foremost in your life. Love them enough to let them become all God intended them to be. Love them enough to let them choose their own paths, even if those paths stray far from your dreams. A family business can be a wonderful experience for everyone involved, or it can be a horrible one. The priorities you set and keep will make the difference for your children.

Pros and Cons

There are both pros and cons to involving your children in your business. Let's take a quick look at the advantages:

1. Teaches your children responsibility. By being involved in your home business, your children will acquire a very rare commodity in today's society: a sense of responsibility.

2. Ensures your children's safety. When your children are working with you, they're safe. At least you know where they are!

3. Teaches your children work skills, good habits, and good values. Involvement in your home business can instill in your children good values, habits, and skills they'll need later in life. You can teach them from a very young age to develop a proper attitude and respect for work.

4. Offers your children an informed career choice. Your children may very well grow up and decide they don't want to follow in your career steps. That's okay. At least they'll have a good idea of what they don't want to do. And along the way, they'll probably develop a much clearer sense of what career they would like to pursue.

5. Avoids the catch-22 after your children graduate. As I mentioned before, most young people face a catch-22 when they graduate from high school or college: They can't get a job without experience, and they can't get experience without a job. When your children go out into that great big, scary world of job hunting, at least they'll have something to show for their first eighteen years on the planet if they've been involved in your home business. Potential employers are bound to give the edge to a teen who has been working in the family business since he was four over the teen who has spent his summers at the beach.

6. Increases your time together as a family. By including your children in your business, you automatically increase the amount of time you spend together. Of course, the quality of that time will depend largely on you—how you conduct your business and how you have raised your children.

7. Provides cheap labor. Okay, I admit it. I really like this advantage. In the old days people had twelve kids just to help run the farm. Maybe they had a good thing going after all. Now if only I could give birth to a graphic designer, an audiovisual specialist, a publicist, and a seminar promoter, my business would have it made!

8. Gives you a flexible resource. Unlike most employees, your children will probably cheer when you tell them there's not enough work to keep them busy for the next month. You can also increase hours when needed, as long as you do so within reason and within state laws.

9. Benefits your successors with on-the-job training. Now remember, there's no guarantee that any of your children will want to take over your business. Please, please, don't force them to follow in your footsteps if it's not the right path for them. However, let's assume that Junior wants to run the business someday. The many years of working alongside you will leave him (or her) in good standing to take over the business when you're ready to retire.

Now let's look at some of the potential downsides of involving your children in your home business:

1. Your children may grow up to resent the business and you. Yes, it's true. Your beloved business may become a curse to your beloved children, especially if you treat your beloved business as though it's *more* *important* than your children. No child wants to play second fiddle to a balance sheet.

2. You may overwork your helpers. Be careful not to overwork your children. It's not right, and again, they may come to resent both you and the business.

3. It can be expensive if you simply make up work for your kids to do. Some of you may have worked for a company where the owner's children made little contribution as workers but drew hefty paychecks anyway. This free-ride syndrome is a trap for children, both young and old. Remember, you do your children no favors by teaching them that the world will give them something for nothing.

4. Your children may feel undue pressure to follow in the family business. Surely we all know someone who has been put in this situation, and it's not enviable. Again, the key is letting your children develop their own natural talents and interests. If those fit in with the future of your business, wonderful. Let them join if they wish.

5. Your children's involvement may create customer-relations problems. Even hard-working children of the boss sometimes get a bum rap. Some people may secretly envy them, thinking they're getting an unfair advantage. On the other hand, if your child needs to learn professionalism, maybe it's time to dish up some tough love.

Caring for Family Members with Special Needs

If you're caring for elderly parents or a disabled family member, you can apply many of the same principles outlined for mothers with children at home. Find creative ways to work when you can and stay radically focused during the time you do have available. A growing trend among home-based workers is intentionally limiting working hours. Many are finding they actually get more done when they work less. Author Timothy Ferriss, in his book *The 4-Hour Work Week*, strongly recommends this approach. Although working only four hours per week seems a bit far-fetched to me, I've personally set a goal of trimming back my work schedule to four hours per day.

Questions ||||||||||||||||||||||||||||||||||||||||||||||||||||||||||||||||||||||||||||||||||||||||||||||||||||||||||||||||||||||||||||||||||||||||||||

1. Which of the techniques for occupying your children do you plan to implement? How and when will you do so?

2. How can you involve your children in your business?

3. Will your children serve as occasional helpers, or do you intend for them to become regular employees?

4. How will you compensate your children?

5. Which of the advantages of involving your children in the business are most significant for you and why?

6. Which of the downsides of involving your children are most significant to you and why? How will you guard against them?

7. If you're a caregiver, how can you adapt some of the concepts presented in this chapter to your particular situation?

Assignments ||||||||||||||||||||||||||||||||||||||||||||||||||||||||||||||||||||||||||||||||||||||||||||||||

1. Create systems for managing your children while you work. Write your notes in the space provided.

2. If you're planning to involve your children in your home business, map out what you envision on a large piece of paper and sit down to discuss your plans with them.

3. Discuss compensation strategies with your spouse or other trusted advisers. Then discuss them with your children.

4. Create systems for managing your caregiving responsibilities, if applicable.

Your Spouse and Your Business

One of the very first things you need to do when you're considering starting a home business is to sit down and discuss the idea with your spouse. Without his support, your business simply cannot succeed. Not only is it important to make sure your husband is on board from the beginning, but it's also important to keep him on board throughout the journey. If at any point your husband begins to resent your business, you'll be in a heap of trouble. No one else on earth is better positioned to either support or undermine your success.

It's a good idea to have a scheduled meeting with your spouse and establish boundaries. This should be done in a large block of time, with no distractions. You'll need to discuss questions like these:

- How many hours per day will you work?
- Will you work evenings?
- What if your husband is tired and doesn't want to watch the children when you have a meeting scheduled? What will your backup plan be?
- Do you plan to work weekends? If you do, will you work every weekend or just one or two weekends per month?

- What will you do if your spouse feels neglected?
- What will you do if your marriage begins to suffer?

It's vitally important for both of you to establish ground rules and expectations regarding your business from the start and to keep the lines of communication open. Remember: Don't lose the forest for the trees. You may want to work from home because your family is a priority. Great! Your marriage is the foundation of that family, and it would be a cruel irony if the home business you start for the sake of your family ends up tearing your family apart instead. It's happened before. Keep your marriage first priority and structure your business around it, not vice versa.

> *Your marriage is the foundation of that family, and it would be a cruel irony if the home business you start for the sake of your family ends up tearing your family apart instead.*

As we discussed in the previous chapter, working more hours isn't always the best way to generate more income. In fact, there's compelling evidence that too many hours devoted to a home business becomes counterproductive. At the very least, there's a law of diminishing returns as exhaustion, boredom, or both set in.

By establishing firm boundaries that honor your spouse, you'll be setting yourself up for greater efficiency and long-term success. So don't resist or resent it if your spouse says, "Thus far and no farther." Work within those guidelines with a cheerful heart and a concentrated mind. I believe that God will bless both you and your business for it.

Working with Your Spouse

What good is it if you've been set free from the bondage of corporate America, but your husband is still trapped? As long as one spouse is tied down to an employer, in a very real sense, both are tied down.

A rapidly growing trend in America is husbands and wives working from home together. Network-marketing companies have long advocated this lifestyle approach and are well structured for couples to begin with one spouse working part-time in a home business, graduating to one spouse full-time at home, and then gradually moving toward both husband and wife working full-time in the business. It's a very appealing option, and many couples enjoy this freedom.

Working together in your own business certainly offers some distinct advantages, such as the ability to live and work anywhere in the world, as well as the opportunity to travel and take vacations anytime you want. Suddenly, every business trip can become a couple's getaway. You can go to fabulous resorts together, and as long as you conduct legitimate business while you're there—voilà!—it's a tax deduction. You've got to love that! Again, many network-marketing companies arrange their conventions in appealing locations for just this reason.

A rapidly growing trend in America is husbands and wives working from home together.

Couples who work together can enjoy more time together, set their own hours, and live by their own values. You can have shared goals and, if you desire, the opportunity to develop a family business that will become a legacy for your children—maybe even your grandchildren.

Potential Pitfalls of Working Together

Of course, on the downside, there are some potential pitfalls when you and your spouse join forces in a home business. First, you may well be putting all of your eggs in one basket, as the saying goes, and if the business fails, it might be financially devastating. Obviously, the ideal approach is for one spouse to maintain a steady paycheck while partnering with the spouse who is totally focused on building the home business to the point where it can sustain both of you full-time.

The biggest complaint I hear from couples who work together is that the business can easily become all-consuming. My advice: Make sure you choose a business that both of you absolutely love, so even if it does take over your lives at times, you won't really mind that much!

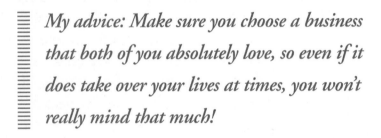

My advice: Make sure you choose a business that both of you absolutely love, so even if it does take over your lives at times, you won't really mind that much!

Another pitfall of working together in a home business is the loss of corporate benefits, such as health insurance and a retirement plan. This shouldn't be taken lightly or shrugged off as something you can deal with "later." Advance planning will be required to ensure a smooth transition toward a paycheck-less family.

And then there are the potential relationship pitfalls of joint business ownership. Working together day in and day out can test the mettle of any marriage. It might enhance your marriage . . . or it might kill the romance, if you're not careful. (That's why I mentioned going to business meetings at those romantic resorts!)

The Top Ten Tips for Working with Your Spouse

Obviously, it's not a decision to be made lightly, but if you and your spouse decide you'd like to follow the path of working together, keep in mind the following guidelines:

1. **Keep marriage and children first.** You don't have to sacrifice success for your family, and you certainly don't have to sacrifice your family for success. When you live according to right priorities, you enjoy a greater potential for success in every area of life.

2. **Respect each other.** Did you ever work with someone who thought the only way to get ahead was by putting everyone else down? Have you ever been guilty of acting that way yourself? If the put-down strategy is one of the skills you picked up in corporate America, now is the time to leave it behind. Successful entrepreneurial couples respect each other, and they go out of their way to demonstrate that respect in public. There is absolutely nothing to be gained by putting down or otherwise disrespecting your mate. But there is much to be gained by praising your spouse publicly and loudly. Mutual respect is key to the health of both your marriage and your bottom line.

3. **Complement each other's talents and carve up turf accordingly.** Isn't it amazing how the very things that attracted you to your partner can sometimes drive you crazy? But when you work together, you'll be reminded just how blessed you are to have a partner with a different set of strengths and weaknesses. If you're going to

succeed—and stay sane—be sure to divide and conquer (the work, that is, not each other!).

4. **Stay supportive of each other.** Since everyone has good days and bad days, one advantage of working together is that *one* of you is usually "up." When your other half is discouraged or has faced a major setback, it's your job as a friend and business partner to be supportive.

5. **Compete with the world outside, not with each other.** I once listened to a husband and wife debating over who had the larger coffee table in his or her corporate office. These two competed with each other on everything. A small dose of competitiveness can actually be healthy, because it motivates both partners to ever higher achievement. Unfortunately, some couples let the competition get totally out of control. The person to beat is not the man or woman sleeping on the other side of the bed; it's the company doing business on the other side of town. Stress cooperation rather than competition.

6. **Laugh.** One woman who works with her husband observed, "My husband knows it's time to get me away from the office when I don't laugh anymore." Did you know numerous studies have revealed a direct correlation between humor and good health? If you haven't been laughing lately, maybe you're overdue for some fun! When you equip your business, don't forget to equip yourself with a healthy sense of humor. As Dwight D. Eisenhower wrote, "A sense of humor is part of the art of leadership, of getting along with people, of getting things done."[1] If you can't think of your own jokes, rent a comedy.

7. **Set clear work-home boundaries.** As with solo home businesses, it's important for a husband-wife home business to
   be kept in proper bounds. That means having a distinct
   work area—perhaps even separate offices for husband
   and wife. Don't allow your home-based business to over-
   take your entire home. In addition to setting specific working hours, you'll need to be steadfast in observing
   not-working hours! One way to ensure that your dream of a
   home business doesn't become a nightmare is to agree,
   in advance, on working hours. You may even decide that
   one spouse will work earlier in the morning and the other
   will work later in the afternoon, so you'll have time together,
   and time to work independently.

8. **Rest.** Take at least one day off per week, and two days off
   whenever possible—one for active fun, one for rest. It's
   especially helpful to get out of the house, out of doors,
   and best of all, out of town occasionally.

9. **Keep your personal and business lives separate.** This is
   easier said than done, but try not to talk about your business constantly at home. While I do want you to be passionate about your business, you and your husband need
   other connections as well. One thing that helps is developing hobbies and common interests that are quite distinct from your business. Take up rock climbing, biking,
   fishing, or some other fun activity. As long as it has
   absolutely nothing to do with your business, it's a winning
   idea!

10. **Reward yourselves.** Set joint goals and celebrate their
    achievement by doing something you both enjoy.

Traveling Spouses

If you have a traveling spouse and no kids at home, you may have lots of time to work while your spouse is gone—except that you may have to do more jobs around the house when you're alone. But when your spouse comes home, well, that's another matter. If your traveler is gone for weeks at a time, there'll be piles of laundry to contend with when he returns. And then there's the catching up and getting reacquainted. Or your spouse may take over in a certain area when he or she is home and doesn't do things your way. What happens to your business plans then?

Again, openly discussing expectations goes a long way. Would your spouse prefer for you to work while he is away and put the business on hold when you both are at home, or at least limit your hours? Only the two of you can decide what works best for your marriage.

If your spouse travels and you have kids in the home, there may be even bigger adjustments. Some children act up for a few days when a parent leaves and again when he or she returns. They may challenge your authority and generally have a hard time adjusting. The great thing about a home business is that you control your own schedule. You can take a few days off or drastically reduce your working hours during those transition days as your spouse comes and goes.

Questions ||||||||||||||||||||||||||||||||||||||||||||||||||||||||||||||||||||||||||||||||||||||||||||||||||

1. Have you sat down with your spouse and clarified expectations, ground rules, and boundaries for your home business? If not, it's past time to do that.

2. What concerns, if any, has your spouse expressed about your decision to work from home? (Or if you're already operating a home business, what issues have come up as a result?)

3. Does the idea of working with your spouse appeal to you?

4. Which of the advantages seemed particularly worthwhile?

5. Which of the pitfalls were of greatest concern?

6. Do you realistically think you and your spouse could work together? Why or why not?

7. What would your ideal work-and-family life look like? Paint a vivid picture.

Aſſignmentſ |||||||||||||||||||||||||||||||||||||||||||||||||||||||||||||||||||||||||||||||||||||||||||||||

1. Sit down with your spouse. Both of you review your expectations regarding a home business. On a separate sheet of paper put the ground rules in writing, including when you will and will not work, and what your spouse is and is not willing to do to support you. Be clear.
2. Discuss the concept of working together from home. If there is preliminary interest, begin to envision what the path might look like. Talk about some first steps to take in that direction. Revisit this chapter every few months to make adjustments.

Godspeed on Your Journey

So there you have it, some practical ideas to help you start a home business and keep it going and growing. Of course, you can't keep doing something until you've made a start. Sometimes beginning is the hardest part of all, because once you get in gear, the laws of momentum kick in and start working on your behalf.

I hope you've worked through the assignments included in the book. If not, now is the time to turn back to page 46 and go through them systematically. This time through, do the hard work of putting pen to paper to develop your strategy for making money from home.

> *I've been privileged to enjoy this wonderful life for twenty years. I know you can do the same, with God's help and your own diligent effort.*

It's my hope and prayer that you'll discover a whole new way of living as you launch your home business. It's a wonderful life, filled with time, freedom, and financial independence. I've been privileged to enjoy this wonderful life for twenty years. I know you can do the same, with God's help and your own diligent effort.

So I leave you with wishes for Godspeed on your journey and a promise to help you along the way in whatever way I can. Remember, you'll find more help at www.makingmoneywithdonna.com ✳. Join me and share your journey.

Notes

Introduction

1. Bruce J. Evensen, "Black Monday Stock Market Crash," *Dictionary of American History* (Farmington Hills, MI: Gale Group, 2003), quoted in Encyclopedia.com, http://www.encyclopedia.com/doc/1G2-3401800470.html (accessed October 1, 2009).

Chapter Two

1. Bill Hibbler and Joe Vitale, *Meet and Grow Rich: How to Easily Create and Operate Your Own "Mastermind" Group for Health, Wealth, and More* (Hoboken, NJ: Wiley and Sons, 2006), 31.

Chapter Three

1. Eric Pace, "Edwin H. Land Is Dead at 81; Inventor of Polaroid Camera," *New York Times,* March 2, 1991, http://www.nytimes.com/1991/03/02/obituaries/edwin-h-land-is-dead-at-81-inventor-of-polaroid-camera.html?pagewanted=all.
2. Charles Thompson, *What a Great Idea!* (New York: Harper-Collins, 1992), 13.

Part II

1. Jack Canfield, Mark Victor Hansen, and Les Hewitt, *The Power of Focus* (Deerfield Beach, FL: Health Communications, 2000).

Chapter Five

1. Paul Edwards, Sarah Edwards, and Peter Economy, *Home-Based Business for Dummies* (Hoboken, NJ: Wiley Publishing, 2005), 45–59.

Chapter Six

1. EBay, "E-Commerce," http://www.ebayinc.com/who (accessed November 2, 2009).

Chapter Seven

1. Zig Ziglar and John P. Hayes, *Network Marketing for Dummies*, (Hoboken, NJ: Wiley Publishing, 2006), 343.
2. Direct Selling Association, "What Is Direct Selling?" http://www.dsa.org/aboutselling/what/ (accessed October 24, 2009).
3. Research carefully before you invest retirement money. Make sure your money is safe. Here are two Web sites with retirement calculators (I'm not recommending the sites' products) that you can experiment with to get an estimation of the amount you need to be investing to reach a certain financial goal by a certain age: http://cgi.money.cnn.com/tools/retirementplanner/retirementplanner.jsp and http://www.moneychimp.com/calculator/retirement_calculator.htm.

Chapter Eight

1. Yanik Silver with Robert Olic, *Moonlighting on the Internet: 5 World-Class Experts Reveal Proven Ways to Make An Extra Paycheck Online Each Month* (Madison, WI: Entrepreneur Press, 2008), 3.
2. Ibid., xxv.

Chapter Eleven

1. Charles Hummel, *The Tyranny of the Urgent* (Downers Grove, IL: InterVarsity, 1967), 8.
2. Ibid., 3.

Chapter Twelve

1. Yanik Silver with Robert Olic, *Moonlighting on the Internet: 5 World-Class Experts Reveal Proven Ways to Make An Extra Paycheck Online Each Month* (Madison, WI: Entrepreneur Press, 2008), 40.

Chapter Seventeen

1. Dwight D. Eisenhower, "Some Thoughts on the Presidency," in *The Power of the Presidency: Concepts and Controversy,* ed. Robert S. Hirschfield (Piscataway, NJ: Transaction Publishers, 2005), 123.

FOCUS ᴼᴺ FAMILY®

Welcome to the Family

Whether you purchased this book, borrowed it, or received it as a gift, we're glad you're reading it. It's just one of the many helpful, encouraging, and biblically based resources produced by Focus on the Family® for people in all stages of life.

Focus began in 1977 with the vision of one man, Dr. James Dobson, a licensed psychologist and author of numerous best-selling books on marriage, parenting, and family. Alarmed by the societal, political, and economic pressures that were threatening the existence of the American family, Dr. Dobson founded Focus on the Family with one employee and a once-a-week radio broadcast aired on 36 stations.

Now an international organization reaching millions of people daily, Focus on the Family is dedicated to preserving values and strengthening and encouraging families through the life-changing message of Jesus Christ.

Focus on the Family MAGAZINES

These faith-building, character-developing publications address the interests, issues, concerns, and challenges faced by every member of your family from preschool through the senior years.

FOCUS ON THE FAMILY THRIVING FAMILY™
Marriage & parenting

FOCUS ON THE FAMILY CLUBHOUSE JR.™
Ages 4 to 8

FOCUS ON THE FAMILY CLUBHOUSE®
Ages 8 to 12

FOCUS ON THE FAMILY CITIZEN®
U.S. news issues

For More INFORMATION

 ONLINE:
Log on to
FocusOnTheFamily.com
In Canada, log on to
FocusOnTheFamily.ca

 PHONE:
Call toll-free:
800-A-FAMILY
(232-6459)
In Canada, call toll-free:
800-661-9800

Rev. 10/09

More Great Resources
from Focus on the Family®

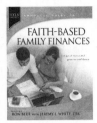

Complete Guide to Faith-Based Family Finances
by Ron Blue and Jeremy White
Whether you're a financial whiz, a financial novice, or somewhere in between, the *Complete Guide to Faith-Based Family Finances* is filled with commonsense tools to help you make wise financial decisions year after year. In addition to covering every area of financial planning, this helpful resource contains the answers to many of the questions asked by families like yours.

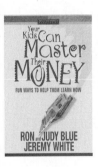

Your Kids Can Master Their Money: Fun Ways to Help Them Learn How
by Ron and Judy Blue and Jeremy White
A kid's perspective on money often doesn't go beyond what it can buy now in the candy aisle of the store. Written by financial advisors Ron and Judy Blue along with Jeremy White, this book shows children how creatively using and saving money can be fun—and rewarding. It's an investment in your children's outlook on finances that will have great payoffs in their adult lives.

Welcome Home: Our Family's Journey to Extreme Joy
by Kimberley Woodhouse
Due to a rare medical disorder, Kayla Woodhouse feels no pain, doesn't sweat, and needs protective cooling gear just to go outside. Millions of people have experienced glimpses of Kayla's life on *Extreme Makeover: Home Edition*. Kimberley Woodhouse, her mom, takes readers behind the cameras to reveal their family's journey. The story demonstrates how, even in tough circumstances, you can shift your life from heartbreak to extreme joy.

FOR MORE INFORMATION

Online:
Log on to FocusOnTheFamily.com
In Canada, log on to focusonthefamily.ca.

Phone:
Call toll free: 800-A-FAMILY
In Canada, call toll free: 800-661-9800.

BPZZXP1